Rethinking the Headlines

Studies in Law, Justice and Society

Joel Clarke Gibbons

VANTAGE PRESS
New York

Cover design by Polly McQuillen

FIRST EDITION

Published by Vantage Press, Inc.
419 Park Ave. South, New York, NY 10016

Manufactured in the United States of America
ISBN: 0-533-15399-9

Library of Congress Catalog Card No.: 2005909996

0 9 8 7 6 5 4 3 2 1

To Crispina, Marcus, Eileen, Hugh, and to all
who love them

Contents

Part Four: Sources of Law: Natural Law, Common Law, and Public Policy

Preface

What does conservative philosophy have to say about all the many aspects of government and civil society? Or in other words, how can one characterize the political science of Conservatism?

This question was first posed by Socrates and by his spokesman Plato, and it has been revisited innumerable times throughout history. If a hundred thinkers were to weigh in on the subject, there is every reason to suppose that the hundred-and-first, reading what went before, would feel absolutely obligated to tackle it again, to apply their insights to prevailing conditions, and occasionally to make up for the oversights of his or her predecessors. Notwithstanding the highly presumptuous title I have chosen, I accept freely that this little book is only one more brick in a wall that I will never see completed.

My title was chosen because consistent conservative thought seems to me to be relegated to the fringe of American intellectual life. Milton Friedman, economist and conservative philosopher, wrote recently that when he was a student, the air was filled with the rhetoric of socialism, although in America the reality was *laissez-faire*. Today, he continued, the air is filled with talk of freedom, but the reality is socialism. Since the ideas have for too long seemed dormant, it is necessary to shake them up. Speak boldly. Think broadly. Make no little mistakes. If this volume were entitled "What Conservative philosophy has to mumble about several moderately interesting subjects," everyone who happened even to pick it up would be fast asleep before he or she had even learned who was the publisher. Consequently, I am authorized to make the following unqualified promise: Any reader who falls asleep two or more times in the course of reading this book is entitled to double his money back. He need only present his sales receipt to me and I will honor it doubled.

One reason that books of this kind—characterizing conservative or progressive philosophy—are rather rare is that there is no agreed definition of those terms. It is very necessary therefore to define them at the start. *Conservatism* is the belief that there are eternal truths that should be allowed to govern the lives of men and women. While the body of truths is immutable, they are not immediately obvious. Study and thought are needed to discern them. As they become revealed however, their impact and their implications become evident also, and from that time our highest calling is to make them effective in human affairs. Some believe, moreover, that in part these truths have been revealed directly by the god who made us—we are religious conservatives—but that is not essential to the idea of conservatism. Most truths are natural truths which are discernable to everyone because they are woven into the natural world and into our nature and our lives. There is a unity of natural and revealed truth—this proposition is of course one of the greatest insights of St. Thomas Aquinas—and so natural law and natural truth are in no way inferior.

The goal of conservative law and political science is to subject lawmaking, jurisprudence, and administration of the civil government to the known body of eternal truth. An objection, or perhaps a caution, may be raised here, that since not all the truths are as yet known, one should be hesitant to apply the partial truth that is known. That proposition however contradicts that concept of truth itself. It is raised for the most part by persons who doubt that there is any truth. In fact, truth *is* actually "true." There is no danger that it will be displaced at some future time.

Progressivism, which proposes a radically different political and legal philosophy, has as its central tenet that the happiness of the public is the highest good, and the law and governance exist to, as much as possible, give the people whatever they want. It is not a logical impossibility that Dr. Pangloss was right: What makes the people happy is precisely to subject themselves willingly to the rights and duties imposed by the immutable truths. I think it is safe to say, however, that practically no progressive believes that. They place the greatest happiness of the greatest number at the center of their philosophy because they do not think there are eternal truths.

Indeed, it is characteristic of progressives that they deny the constancy of truths. They assert rather that the world is continually changing and that the old and comfortable have no more claim on us than does the latest innovation. New or old alike, if it is what the people seem at the moment to want, it is good *ipso facto.* It is quite understandable that progressive philosophy attaches a uniquely high importance to peace in society. Conflicts arise about what it is that people want, and progressivism affords no basis on which to resolve such conflicts because in theory any one of the contending desires could be the greater good for the greater number. Faced with really irreconcilable differences—the conflict between religious radicalism and secularist fundamentalism that bubbles so hotly today—progressivism is stumped. If everyone were to join the Wahhabi fanatics, the problem would be solved, and on the other hand if everyone were willing to sing from the French national hymnal everything would be just fine too. Within the logic of progressivism, the problem is not how I, the progressive, would choose. The problem is that they, the public, are unable to choose. If only everyone would just stop fighting about it. Conflicts of this sort actually illuminate the logical flaws of the progressivism as a philosophy. It is unable to govern, to deal with such basic conflicts.

It is not, however, my commission either to present or to dispatch the progressive position on law and justice and society. My point is merely to explain a familiar practical difference between progressives and conservatives, which is that conservatives are far more comfortable with the imposition of rules, even by force. The reader will detect throughout this book that I accept the legitimacy of imposed rules and the legitimacy of those institutions—jails and prisons, courts, police—that exist to implement them. I do not think that my assumption will be highly controversial. Almost everyone but the purest of progressive thinkers accepts them as necessary and legitimate.

As different as are conservatism and progressivism, there is a third "ism" that entirely differs from both although it is sometimes confused with conservatism. That -ism is fascism. There is nothing conservative about fascism. Far from postulating eternal truths, it posits that the greatest good is whatever the governor wants. Fascism inevitably results in a lot of imposition of decisions and rules by the authorities, because the desires of the governor are so often in conflict with the desires of the governed. So let me state unequivocally at the start, to the chagrin of fascists,

The state is not the font of eternal truth.

Organization of This Book

This book consists of chapters that I have grouped into four general headings: the criminal law, law and human rights, marriage and divorce, and natural law. The book has grown out of the individual chapters that were at one time separate essays that I composed on specific topics. The five chapters on the criminal law and the penal code were written over the course of about five years, from 2000 to 2005. As luck would have it, even though they were composed separately, the treatment of the subject naturally evolved in a way that made it very easy to assemble them into a longer piece. The other chapters appeared over the course of the same years.

While this then constitutes a set of essays that should be both provocative and insightful, it is obviously not and is not intended to be a comprehensive survey of law and society. Many subjects are touched and many equally important ones are left unmentioned. It is my modest hope that anyone who reads it will have gained a deeper appreciation of the conservative philosophy as it applies to law and government, and that armed with this knowledge, will be able to apply it in all the innumerable other matters that arise.

The thoughts expressed and the logic by which they stand or fall can only be judged by the results. On each topic that I have raised, I have endeavored to apply a consistent philosophical premise—conservatism—to the realities as they exist today. One may understandably be inclined to ask on what premise do I assert that I have anything of value to say? In the world today we are taught to look for and to ask for visible credentials. On matters of law, we look to lawyers, and to thinkers with legal credentials. On politics we look for credentials in the field of political science, and so on. I, perhaps shockingly, do not claim any such credentials. Those who rely on them will no doubt put away this book, filled with a sense of scandal that just an ordinary citizen, someone like themselves, would presume to write on recondite matters.

My answer for that person is to pause and take a deep breath. Do not be afraid to look and to think. If what I have written is false, then let its errors be seen and corrected. But if what I write is true and informative, then what further credential do I need?

To carry the point a bit further, however, let me explain that I do not live in a cave nor was I raised by wolves. I hold a doctorate in mathematics from Northwestern University and I hold both an M.B.A. and a doctorate in business from the University of Chicago. While a student at the University of Chicago, I had the good fortune to spend a couple of years serving as an assistant to Prof. Isaac Ehrlich. The very first chapter of this book is also the first of these essays historically, and it was written to respond to friends and colleagues who wanted a single summary of his research and of its implications for the penal code. My legal qualifications are further buttressed by the year that I spent at the law school of the University of Chicago. Besides this little book, I have written and published in the fields of mathematics, economics, and finance. In addition, I was for about fifteen years a trader in Chicago, including eight years as an independent local trader.

The name Logistic Research & Trading Co. first came into being as the corporate umbrella under which I did business as a trader. It is no longer an active business, but for so many years I promoted it among clients and prospects, as well as on the street, so that it has become almost a kind of alter ego. It is now as familiar as old socks, and so I hope I will be forgiven for perpetuating it.

Author's Note

My first exposure to the philosophical work of Thomas Aquinas was in college, where three years of philosophy were required of all students. Since that time I have grown in my appreciation for his insights, as I have seen them in practice in many fields, and have found his ideas illuminating every time. This is especially true in the fields of law and government.

Looking around the intellectual and legal landscape of America today, I see confusion and disarray: a lack of clear thought; a lack of grounded reason; the absence of time-tested principle. Patrick Buchanan, who preceded me by a few years at Georgetown, has written recently that there are no conservatives anymore in Washington, that conservatism is dead. I understand his frustration, but luckily for me I come to this issue fresh and unbloodied. While my short book of essays is not going to start a revolution, I hope and I believe that it may have some small impact to reintroduce seasoned troopers like myself and fresh student minds also to the bedrock of conservative political thought.

Part One

Justice, Deterrence, and the Penal Code

1

On Justice and Deterrence: The Case of Capital Punishment

The authority given to the government to punish criminals is unlike any other capacity or function that the government wields. Every other task that a government undertakes is generally easily related to the duty of the government and those who govern to serve the interest of the entire nation or state without discriminating among the citizens. The pomp and circumstance that leaders are invested with and the perquisites of office often tax this relationship, but everyone agrees that good servants of the public deserve their rewards, and the public usually endorses, even enthusiastically, the prestige and honors that come with public office. It is the authority to punish that rests uneasily on the plan of government and that demands the full attention of an entire police and court system.

Specifically, the controversy that swirls around the death penalty can never, it seems, be put to rest. The moral and the practical issues are understandably debated over and over again. Our reluctance to exact the penalty of death is by no means new. The Athenian state had stopped all executions at the time of Socrates, and only his stubborn refusal to submit to any other punishment forced his death. It is of course the mark of Athens's greatness that she placed the lives of her citizens above the convenience of the State. As much as I also admire this rule, I will argue in this essay that the death penalty is acceptable and legitimate and I will explore both the conditions under which that is true, and the conditions that moderate or constrain the practice. These matters go directly to the heart of the criminal law itself and the administration of justice, and they are essentially moral questions. So we have to ask ourselves, what is the moral basis for the criminal law and for the punishing of criminals?

Because the moral law deals with actualities—the actual consequences of what people do and the actual conditions that motivate their actions—it is always practical. To begin, we may start with two practical questions. First, how do we reach such a decision and carry out the verdict of death, and second, does the threat of execution actually deter criminals and therefore spare their victims?

Due Process

The demands of due process impose all kinds of limits on the criminal law in all cases. Standards of proof and of evidence, the provision of legal counsel to all defendants, public access to the proceedings, the right of appeal, and so on, are all designed to implement due process. These are not specific to capital trials, of course, but in the case where the verdict may be death there is an unusual, added condition imposed by due process. It arises when we ask whether execution is different from other punishments.

Life in prison, long years of forced labor, long periods

of solitary confinement—all of these can be associated with prison. Separation from one's family, fines so onerous that they impoverish even a rich person and reduce him to misery also—these are all hard punishments. Society cannot easily justify using any of them. Death is unique however in that the state takes from the person even the opportunity to repent and change. Due process requires that the sentence of death be imposed in a way that does not diminish, but if possible encourages, acceptance of guilt and remorse. Long terms in prison do not seem to encourage repentance and change, or else it would not be a truism that everyone in the penitentiary is innocent. One of the defenses of the death penalty in the past was that for these persons, for murderers and similar persons, only the knowledge that they were about to die would cause them to accept their guilt.

It may be objected at this point that this is the twenty-first century, and we do not hold such a moralistic view of the criminal law, or of life at all. One may say that "we do not care if the murderer repents, because we do not recognize repentance." Be that as it may, it overlooks the point at issue here, which is whether the death penalty unjustly deprives a person of the opportunity to repent. Only if there were no morality or repentance would this issue simply not arise. Where however repentance is deemed a good in itself, the penal system must be reconciled with the implications of that good.

In any case, what is at issue here is what constitutes due process in these cases. Clearly, the law must allow a period of time to elapse between the rendering of a verdict and the execution. Summary execution is always wrong under the law. The convicted person must be given time to think about the verdict of the court and about why that verdict was reached. If a guilty man still rejects the evidence of his guilt and the justness of the verdict, he is in the end free to do so. It cannot be better to keep him like an animal in prison for years or decades in hopes that he will change. It is the duty of the law and of the courts to fix a reasonable period for anyone sentenced to death and never to act hastily, but having done so, and having made any other practical provisions to encourage repentance, it is not the duty of the state to keep the convict alive indefinitely in the fond hope that atonement is just around the corner.

So due process demands that every reasonable provision be made to promote repentance and contrition. If this is not observed in practice, then it would be true that the death penalty does deprive the person of the opportunity to repent.

A second argument is sometimes advanced against the finality of execution, and that is that no correction can be made for a faulty verdict. If it should be proved that the convict is in fact innocent, then he can be freed from prison but not from the grave. This line of reasoning is literally correct but it is nonetheless not relevant. If there is reason to think that the person is actually innocent, he should be acquitted. It will be small consolation after he has been caged up for most of his life to release him to live out his days wholly alienated from society and a virtual hermit. If a prisoner is proved innocent, he must of course be freed immediately no matter what his condition, but this is not something to plan for and to hope for. This line of reasoning does not actually invoke a rule of due process. It instead proposes that there is never due process, that we never know who is innocent and who is guilty. If that were true, we should simply acquit everyone and close down the courts. Or rather, we should get better police. It is not an argument about justice. Any person or any legal process that is incapable of coming to a final determination about facts and evidence is actually incapable of deciding justly.

The death penalty is unique in both its terror and in its finality. It is the most terrifying form of punishment both for those subject to it and for the society that exacts it. It is also final and unchangeable. For these reason it imposes extra demands on due process, as I set forth here. But in other respects execution is no different from other punishments. All punishments are harsh and all entail drastic infringement on the freedoms of the person subjected to them. Long prison terms in particular are exceptionally onerous punishment, leaving the person almost incapable of living in civil society thereafter. As long as the high standards of due process are met, both as to high standards of proof of guilt and to allowance for repentance, then the death penalty is not fundamentally different from any other punishment.

Deterrence: Empirical Evidence

Does the threat of death deter persons from crime? Common sense attests that it does. Informal observation supports this. The evidence that persons accused of capital crimes try at all costs to avoid this sentence certainly confirms that they are not indifferent to the threat of execution. No one disputes these facts, but whether the threat of death deters remains controversial. The only definitive evidence of deterrence has to be behavioral: evidence based on how the frequency of capital crime actually responds to the threat of execution. The alternative, which is speculation based on the psychology of criminals, does not and cannot properly account for the diversity of people. At the end of the day, some persons will be deterred by the threat of death and others will not. There is no single psychological analysis that applies to all of even to most of the cases. The effectiveness of the death penalty has to be judged therefore by its results in the aggregate. If it lowers, for example, the murder rate a great deal, that is all that anyone could ask. If on the other hand it has almost no perceptible effect on the murder rate, then evidently it is not a deterrent. There are certainly criminals who would not be deterred by the threat of death, just as there are others who are very acutely sensitive to it.

What actually matters is how many of the latter persons there are, and whether this sanction is imposed as a credible threat. It is easy to overlook the fact that whether the death penalty is in fact an effective deterrent depends not only on the psychology of potential criminals, but also depends on how this punishment is actually imposed. This caveat raises a host of practical considerations about the credibility of the threat, but one is of such overriding importance that it demands to be made explicit here. The death penalty will deter persons from crime only if they connect the risk of execution with the crime. The potential criminal must accept the judgments of guilt and innocence reached by the courts of law. If criminals were to think—rightly or wrongly—that courts convicted the innocent with the guilty and acquitted the guilty with the innocent, then no threatened punishment would deter them. They would see that it would make no difference whether they were guilty or innocent. The threat of any punishment deters only to the degree that the guilty are more likely to be punished than the innocent are, for then there is safety in preserving one's innocence. I owe this observation to Prof. Isaac Ehrlich, whose pioneering research on deterrence and the death penalty still stands as a landmark on this topic. Subsequent research along the lines that he laid down has broadened and deepened his conclusions.[1]

The question Professor Ehrlich addressed is whether there is behavioral evidence that the death penalty does on balance deter murder in America. The question is, as explained, one of practical effect and calls for a judgement of degree. In its purest form, the question asks how many fewer murders there will be as the result of a single, representative execution. It will never be possible to attach an exact number to this question, but his statistical methods provide very important estimates. On the basis of a nationwide sample covering the years from the early '30s to the early '70s, he estimated that the average execution in America in those years deterred eight murders. Subsequent research using state-by-state data reinforced his conclusions in a qualitative way, and actually resulted in a much larger estimated deterrent. The interstate cross section of data, which was taken from the censuses of 1950, 1960 and 1970, provided an estimate of sixteen fewer murders as a result of the average execution. Both estimates are highly significant in a statistical sense, which means that if more data was collected from the same environment that generated this actual data, it is highly unlikely that the new data would lead to a different conclusion.

Estimates like these, based on actual collective behavior, are by their nature conditional on the legal and social circumstances that applied in America during those years. This is true of any kind of behavioral measurement. As I explained before, the finding of an effective deterrent implies among other things that potential murderers accepted the justice of the court verdicts that

9

sentenced persons to death. If the public had doubted that the convicted were actually guilty, there could not have been any deterrent. If in some other place or some other time this acceptance was not present, then in that time and place there would be no deterrent. Similarly, the finding of deterrent value implies that a great many potential murderers were rational enough to weigh their actions and to avoid committing murder. If in some other place or at some other time the public was generally overcome with an irrational passion to murder, deterrence would to some degree be lost. Within the sample at hand however these empirical questions have been answered. It is no longer appropriate to speculate that American criminals of those days were irrational and pathologically bloodthirsty, nor is it necessary to question whether the public generally accepted the justice of the police and courts. The evidence settles those matters.

There are two further important questions addressed by Prof. Ehrlich's research. We cannot really appreciate the significance of his work without understanding them also, because they are what give confidence that the estimates cited above really attached to the risk of execution. One of these companion questions relates to verifying that the estimates relate to cause and effect: to the result caused by an execution for murder. There are in principle other links between the number of murders and the number of executions. During times when the murder rate is high for other reasons, the police and courts are likely to be somewhat overwhelmed. There are likely to be more executions—demanded by a somewhat panicky public—but a lower rate of execution because the resources of courts and police are stretched thin. In other words, at these times it is likely that a murderer runs a lower risk of being executed for his crime. This link also gives a negative correlation between the risk of execution for murder and the murder rate, and could potentially masquerade as deterrence. There are still other potential links too, but this is the only one that gives rise to a negative correlation between the execution and murder rates. Could the empirical finding that they are negatively correlated be the result of this reverse causation? Professor Ehrlich addressed this question of causality directly by using as the rate of execution a rate that applied when the crime was committed, and not using the one that applied after the murderer was convicted. Deterrence posits that it is the anticipated risk of execution that deters, while if causation is reversed, it is the actual murder rate that causes the subsequent risk of execution.

The other complicating factor to address is that of separating the effect of execution for murder from the effects of other determinants of the murder rate. No one supposes that the risk of execution is the only determinant of the murder rate, or of the rate of any other crime. The finding that execution deters specifically assumes that deterrence is marginal to whatever would otherwise be the murder rate. Deterrence only posits that other things being equal, a decision to execute more convicted murderers reduces the murder rate from what it would otherwise be. Even if there were no death penalty, the murder rate would not be 100 percent—not everyone would be a murderer—and similarly if executions for murder were the rule, there would still be murders.

The other determinants are of two general types: the effect of other penal deterrents and the effect of other social and economic factors that apply at the time. It is possible to be rather specific about what are the other deterrents. Professor Ehrlich used three of them: the risk of being arraigned for murder, and the risk of being convicted given arraignment, and the average length of time spent in prison for those who were convicted but not executed. All of these deterrents are also effective, as his statistics clearly show, and quantitatively the most powerful one is the risk of arraignment. If we can hold the other factors constant in practice, raising the risk of arraignment would empirically have the most dramatic effect for lowering the murder rate.[2]

While the other deterrent factors are rather easy to specify, the universe of social and economic factors is correspondingly obscure. Unemployment, poverty, and hopelessness—however that may be measured—all contribute to crime of all kinds and especially to murder. Putting people to work, alleviating poverty and hopelessness, and instilling confidence in the future all lower the incidence of all crimes. No one claims to have perfect empirical measure of these factors, but Professor Ehrlich has expressly controlled for them to the degree possible. He finds for instance that the rate of unemployment and the average age of the population—violent crime is an activity of the young—have very clear empirical correlation with the murder rate in his studies.

The estimated deterrent of the threat of execution is then specifically the effect that can be assigned to the rate of executions, holding both other deterrent factors and other socioeconomic factors constant. As I have emphasized previously, the actual estimate is not in any sense a universal constant. Even if Professor Ehrlich had had an unlimited amount of data to use, so that his estimate was almost perfectly precise in a statistical sense, the fact that it is conditioned on the legal, social, and economic environment that prevailed in America between 1930 and 1975 implies that the numerical estimates cannot be applied to other times and other places. What remains true, however, is that he has documented a place and a period of time when the deterrent of capital punishment was very large. The time and place, moreover, are by no means remote or peculiar. It would require an heroic commitment to a very implausible proposition—that the threat of death does not cause people to think twice and to avoid this risk—to reject the evidence that these studies by Professor Ehrlich and subsequent studies seem to have found.

Thus far I have dealt with two questions that arise often in regard to the death penalty: that it is cruel and unusual and that it is not a deterrent. It is indeed terrifying, the most terrible of all punishments, but it is not a *per se* violation of due process, and it does deter murder and thus save lives.

Deterrence in the Criminal Law

These two propositions, which are of an essentially practical nature, do not address the larger matter of what the demand for justice requires of the sanctions that our criminal courts levy against persons convicted of crime. The morality and the justice of the criminal law rests on deterrence. By deterrence I mean the power of punishments to discourage other persons from committing crimes.

This becomes evident when we consider why we have criminal law instead of relying entirely on private actions of the citizens to defend their own rights. The criminal law and the tort law are alike in that they are ways of addressing infringements of the right of persons. The law expressly allows, moreover, for other relationships of control or authority designed to ensure the interests of persons. The owner of a shop has certain powers over his employees. He can dismiss them essentially at will, and the law will back him up. What is different about the cases that fall under the umbrella of the criminal code, as distinct from civil torts and breaches of contractual duties?

The criminal law is needed in two sorts of cases: those in which one party has so great and threatening a power over others that the weak could not in fact secure their own rights, and those in which the victim could not generally identify the offender or bring him to justice. The latter case includes murder, in which the victim is rendered powerless and entirely without rights of any kind. The civil remedies of tort and contract law are calibrated to compensate for the harm done to the complainant because in these situations that is all he is entitled to. It is the responsibility of the victim to secure his own rights in these cases because that is feasible for him to do so. The criminal law comes into play in cases where the victim cannot feasibly defend his own rights. Very often this inability arises because it is difficult to determine the guilt of the offender. An example: if your employee accidentally shatters the front window of your store you can dock his wages, but if an anonymous vandal throws a brick in the dead of night, there is nothing that you, the shopkeeper, can do about it. It is therefore a given of the criminal law—of the sort of cases that are assigned to the criminal law—that it is very hard to know who is responsible, and that many or most of the time the offender will go unpunished.

The criminal code is needed precisely for this reason: to restrain harms that are almost impossible to prevent, and where the offender is very likely to evade any sanctions. This is of course precisely the fact situation that demands punishments that deter, because a regime of compensation is insufficient. This, as a sidelight, is one reason that it is appropriate that the standard of proof of criminal guilt should be placed rather high in all cases. Since the criminal code assumes that guilt is difficult to discern, the officers of law enforcement cannot rightly complain that the law leaves them with a high standard of proof. If many offenders get off free because of this standard, then that is just another reason that the punishments are chosen for deterrence.

Deterrence is a form of making an example of the criminals who happen to get caught and convicted. It is a given that in some sense they are punished not only for their own crimes but also for the crimes of others who managed to escape punishment. As a result, the convict is also a kind of victim. He is a victim of the imperative of deterrence. While the criminal law rightly refuses to recognize it, there is something honorable and sacrificial in taking punishment. At a human level all convicts deserve our sympathy. This does not change the fact that criminal sanctions must deter; it is rather only a consequence of that fact.

Criminal sanctions are also designed to disable the convicted person himself, wholly apart from deterring other potential offenders. This is also entirely legitimate of course, and one can imagine circumstances where violence and lawlessness are so widespread that it would be enough just to disable the few who are caught and convicted. The wild west of cattle rustlers and claim jumpers might be such an example. Even in such times and places, however, criminal penalties also deter. It quickly becomes obvious to everyone that disabling criminals would simply be too costly and ineffective, and that unless the punishments also deter, they and the society itself will simply fail. The criminal law is therefore made necessary precisely because there are many cases in which someone abuses the rights of another in ways that the victim cannot defend himself and where compensation alone would be either insufficient or unavailable. These are the situations in which the public has to have an armed force in reserve, and must rely on the deterrent of any punishment it metes out.[3]

These are the important, practical considerations that both justify deterrence, and that place it in the context of the criminal law. They do not, however, address the essential moral underpinning of deterrence. The criminal law and its sanctions are not justified as a convenience to the public or as a highly popular public service. What, we ask, is the justice of the criminal law and of deterrence? It rests on this truth, that we cannot as a matter of law sacrifice the innocent in order to preserve the guilty. The law is just to the extent that it defends the innocent, even when it must punish the guilty for that reason.

Deterrence and Revenge

Many critics of the death penalty mistakenly confuse deterrence and revenge. These critics often seem in fact to think that all criminal sanctions are revenge against the criminal by an outraged public. Nothing could be further from the truth. The criminal law, which these persons assume to be an engine of revenge, in fact is society's self-defense against revenge. The criminal law is the tool that the society needs to prevent a rule of revenge for wrongs. It is the tort law that is ironically a highly regulated vehicle of revenge, in the sense that the plaintiff is able to exact compensation for a wrong against him or her. Retribution is feasible and it is just precisely to the extent that there is an objective basis for the amount of the compensation. Civil awards that provide for a deterrent—treble damages for instance—cannot be justified. Only the criminal law has the authority to impose sanctions as deterrent. The civil courts are provided precisely for cases in which compensation is an adequate remedy. It seems to me that punitive damages are the work of a greedy plaintiff bar and legislators that cannot stand up to them despite the clear demands of justice and law.

The genius of the criminal code, and particularly of the sentencing and punitive aspects, is that the rules are set not by the particular victims of a crime, but by society as a whole. They are set, therefore, not to exact revenge but for their deterrent. The difference lies in who it is that fixes punishments for wrongs. Revenge is a regime in which the offended party himself fixes the terms of the punishment. This legitimizes whatever motives the victim feels, including the desire for vengeance. Deterrence is a regime of criminal sanctions in which the society as a whole fixes punishments, and does so not out of spite towards any particular criminal but toward the end of maintaining the rule of law. The community applies a calculus that the victim would not.

An example makes this point. Consider purse snatching, and imagine that a sentence of one year would lessen the number of purses snatched by 20 percent, two years would lower it by 40 percent, and fifteen years would lower it by 90 percent. All of these figures assume all other things equal. Quite reasonably the community might find a 20 percent reduction too small, and a fifteen-year sentence for snatching purses too harsh and too costly. They would settle for the 40 percent improvement if it could be achieved with a comparatively modest cost of a prison term of two years. Why is this not revenge? It is entirely different from revenge in that the identity of the purse snatcher and the identity of any particular victim should have no bearing on the decision. The decision is made not by victims as a group, but by the whole community.

There has been a regrettable tendency in recent years that goes by the name of "victim's rights." It is obviously good and right for the law to extend some extra care and support to victims, but often what goes by this name is actually to bring the particular victim of a crime into the sentencing for that crime. That is an unacceptable opening for a regime of revenge that has no place in the court of law. It is precisely what the criminal law was created to supplant. Revenge is always unjust. This version of so-called "victim's rights," moreover, places the interests of one citizen—the victim—above those of another citizen—the criminal—in a way that violates the duty of equal protection. The criminal then becomes also a victim, and he or his associates may be inclined to exact revenge of their own. Revenge is always wrong because the goal of the law is to reduce harms and to heal conflicts. It is said that the good that a person does lives on long after him, but the evil is buried with his bones. Only by revenge does the evil acquire a life after death.

The legitimacy of a law which reflects the norms and judgments of the society as a whole is recognized not only in the criminal law, but is actually the foundation of all our law. It is invoked throughout the law in the so-called "Reasonable Person" standard. The Reasonable Person is a kind of ideal representative of the community to whom we impute the standards of behavior in all areas. The Reasonable Person is not the average person. The Reasonable one is more ideal, more fair, more anything that we would want the law to be, than is the average person. But the Reasonable Person is a real person, and not an angel. The significance of this standard in this context is simply, however, that it is objective and impersonal. It signifies a whole process of community decisions on standards of behavior and of justice in which we come to agree on how we would want our neighbors to treat us and which standards we are willing to submit our behavior to. In the end, the Reasonable Person is the ultimate judge in every court, and that is how it should be. The sentencing decision is only one example of this.

The Sentencing Decision: Conditions That May Indicate the Death Penalty

Following upon these observations, it must be clear that the sentencing decision always belongs to the judgment and discretion of the community. This is true both as it applies to general sentencing decisions, like whether to provide for the death penalty for a particular class of felonies, and as it applies to individual cases. It is always with the authority of the community—or of their representatives—to commute any sentence in any particular case. The first rule, therefore, for sentencing is that the death sentence is *never* mandatory either for a particular class of crimes or as the punishment for a particular crime.

Having said that, it follows that my opinion, or the opinion of any other individual, is never the standard for fixing the penalty for any sort of crime. My remarks on this point will stand or fall on their own, depending on whether they appear fair and just or unfair and unjust.

19

Their value, such as it is, is purely advisory and informative. There is no rule of law or of justice that mandates any particular penalty for any particular crime, either in general or in a specific case.

There are two conditions that I can identify which make the death penalty a reasonable punishment. The first of these arises in cases where the society is in effect under siege or at war, and where the risk that a lesser punishment might be insufficient to deter is too great. Remember the near total breakdown of law and order in the old West in which every person had to think about self defense all the time. There was no freedom to experiment with alternative approaches to deterrence. Many criminals were, in any case, sent to prison instead of being hanged, but the immediacy of the threat to everyone justified execution of murderers in my opinion. Other cases of the failure of law and order are not hard to find, and I do not mean to set this extreme example as any sort of test. What is in my opinion necessary is that the society reasonably see itself in a virtual state of war against some form of violent crime.

In my opinion, a more recent example has been the situation in poor urban ghettoes, where the ordinary citizens have been terrorized by a clique of powerful criminal organizations financed by drug money. The circumstances of the majority of the poor in their neighborhoods was not appreciably different than if their neighborhoods had been conquered by the Mongol horde or by the Nazis. It was and is the duty of the broader society to come to their defense, and to do so decisively and without delay. It is the great tragedy of those neighborhoods that the same criminals that oppressed them controlled the political organization too, and were for a long time very successful in diverting attention away from helping the victims. It is highly ironic, and it certainly reflects no credit on us, that the criminals often succeeded in painting themselves as the victims!

There are other cases in which it is a particular form of murder that threatens to become epidemic, and against which the society is thus potentially at war. The murder of children and infants, murder by high tech military weapons, murders carried out against a particularly vulnerable component of the community—so-called "hate crimes"—are all instances in which the death penalty might be justified. The common thread in these cases, to repeat an earlier remark, is that the consequences of failing to deter be very grave and that we lack confidence in lesser punishments. We should bear in mind, in any case, that as in the old West, we are not talking about executing all offenders. Most of them will in any case be sent to prison. What is at issue is whether *any* will be executed for their crimes.

The other setting in which I think execution can be justified arises only rarely but in very notorious cases. There is a moralistic or purgative aspect to execution that is not nearly as present in any other sanction. It seems to me that there are crimes so horrible that it is right for the society to reaffirm itself by this means. I am thinking of the kind of mass killers—Richard Speck, John Wayne Gacy, Bluebeard—whose crimes defy almost the very humanity that we profess. Always keeping in mind that every criminal must be given a fair chance to repent his crimes, these cases call for a resounding repudiation by the community as a whole in an almost ritualistic way. This is, despite my general thesis, not a matter of deterrence. We really do not care whether the next Bluebeard will think twice or even three times about what he is about to do. It is small consolation that, if we catch him, at least there will be one fewer Bluebeard, period. That, to my mind, is the kind of society we want to be, one that is just plain intolerant of mindless killers in our midst. These are cases—rare cases—in which it is precisely our commitment to the value of human life that demands a sentence of death.[4]

Actually, criminals of this sort seem almost never to be executed, but live out their appointed years in penitentiary. If that is what the society wants to do, it is their prerogative—as I asserted previously—but it is small mercy to the criminal. Since even the prison system has no means to deal with or help these persons, they are simply incapacitated with drugs and left to spend their days in a drugged stupor. Then at least they are not a danger to the other inmates. That solves the warden's problem, but I cannot see that it does anything for anyone else.

The foregoing remarks can readily be summarized in one general rule. The death penalty is warranted in cases where a particular kind of grave crime—murdering, kidnapping, or the like—threatens not only the specific victim, but threatens the foundations of civil society as well. It is called for in cases where the failure to deter risks provokes a chain reaction of violent self-defense or a breakdown of trust and civility among the public. This arises especially in categories of crime that set particular classes of citizens against each other. The reason that death is warranted in cases of the most heinous crimes is that in these rare cases it is appropriate for the public to express its moral sense in the strongest possible terms, as a sort of communal, public affirmation of common values. This never applies to criminals whose crimes are simply unpopular. That is not deterrence; it is a lynch mob. The category of heinous crimes must be settled in advance without reference to any specific case. It was for that reason that I took the example of Bluebeard.

Having emphasized strongly that death is never mandatory, it is incumbent on me to reiterate the complementary truth that it is the community's judgement to exact the death penalty. They are not free to do so capriciously, but it is their call. Only the community as a whole can know which offences strike so deeply against the foundations of the society that death is a just sanction. This judgement, moreover, is not cast in stone. It depends upon the circumstance of the society—whether for instance they are threatened by neighboring countries or by internal dissension—and it depends upon the frequency of the particular crime. If for instance murder is a rare event, the death penalty would never be justified because no one reasonably feels that the stability of society is endangered by it. Correspondingly, when some form of any grave crime becomes sufficiently common, even the penalty of death may be justified.

Fairness and Equal Treatment

The rule that every sentence meted out reflect the public will implies that inequality of sentences will be the rule and will in fact be an essential characteristic. This is not actually a controversial proposition. In the matter of disparity in sentencing guidelines for different crimes, we readily see that it as being demanded by justice, and not as flouting it. It would be a strange sort of justice that fixed equal sentences for auto theft and treason. Quite the contrary, we accept that the sentencing guidelines are decided by the society to serve its needs, and that this provides for a high degree in disparity in the rules. The same is true of individual cases. The pubic is not usually directly involved in individual sentences, but many parties that decide for the public—both courts of appeal and ultimately the chief executive who has the authority to commute sentences or to pardon—have extraordinary discretion provided by the law. It often happens, moreover, that the cause of prisoners sentenced to death is taken up by various advocates and their cases are reheard in the streets or in the news media. Lastly—but in a sense "firstly"—the case was submitted to a jury of citizens who are supposed to reflect the model of the Rational Person.

The fact that the death penalty, in particular, is targeted at crimes that present a particularly urgent problem introduces sentencing disparities that will inevitably be controversial but that are actually required by justice. The most notable disparity of this kind is the one between treatment of men and women who are convicted for murder. A woman runs a much smaller risk of being sentenced to death for murder than does a man. The reason is that murders committed by women both in the number killings and the kinds, are simply not pressing social problems. We are not by any stretch locked into a war with women as in some settings we are locked into a war with men. This could change, particularly in the area of infanticide, but it is not surprising that today there is little or no demand to execute women who have been convicted of murder. The special treatment of criminals deemed to be "insane" is perhaps an even greater disparity. In any case, the examples of inequality in sentencing are not merely superficial or trivial, but cut right across the criminal code.

The need for equal treatment of the law does apply a restraint on the degree of inequality that can be allowed.

More importantly, it establishes a high standard that must be met to justify disparities. Differences in sentencing arising from attributes of the criminal that do not bear on his guilt—that do not make his crime more or less serious or make him more or less guilty—clearly violate the sixteenth amendment.

The Sentencing Decision: Factors That Militate Against the Death Penalty

There are many reasons—some practical and some more philosophical—that limit the use of the death penalty, and that more generally lift the harshness of criminal sanctions.

Two practical considerations are especially significant. One of these is that the whole regime of sanctions has to provide for incremental deterrence. If the punishment for stealing a loaf of bread was death, there would be a lot less theft of bread no doubt, but there would also be more bloody shootouts in the bakery section of the supermarket. Since there is no sanction beyond death, there is no further deterrence that can be applied. A second practical consideration has to do with the job of the police. It is not easy to arrest suspects who may face a sentence of death. If the risk of that outcome is small, this is not such a big problem, but if death is nearly certain following conviction, the suspect will fight rather than submit. For this reason police are as a group in favor of moderating sentences. The police do always wield an even more powerful deterrent, which is the threat of immediate death, but no one wants this outcome.

The principal philosophical factor is the one I cited at the start of this essay, which is the commitment we expect of our governors to place the value of the individual at the center of the law. The criminal law exists to defend individual persons and their rights from harm. It is actually a violation of that goal for the law to dwell upon or take satisfaction from the gravity of the punishments to be meted out. The law against murder in particular is put in place to save life, not to take it. The reality of deterrence is for that reason the moral underpinning of all criminal sanctions—as I have already argued—but even deterrence is not a desirable end in itself. Most citizens are understandably made uncomfortable by an excessively ruthless criminal code because it smacks of a tyranny imposed from above rather than a regime of defense of human values. The citizens of Athens in Socrates's day—to return to an earlier example—were by no means averse to violence. They happily sent their army and navy off to a ruinous war of world conquest. But they resisted strenuously the thought that the same state that dispatched the army had the authority to put a citizen to death, because they started from the premise that the state exists to serve the citizens.

Conclusion

I would like to conclude this short essay with a very current example that may carry an important lesson for a public that must make these decisions about criminal sanctions. The example involves remission of punishment. Whether any other community wishes to imitate it or to dismiss it is something that I do not pretend to know.

The example is the treatment of Protestant and Catholic paramilitaries in Ulster. As a part of the establishing of peace in that province, a great many prisoners have been released from prison even though many of them were convicted of the most serious crimes. It is necessary to start this account by reviewing the historical perspective. As the result of centuries of English rule, Irish society was split between native Irish—resisters of English rule—and Scots Irish. Until about two centuries ago these factions got along pretty well, and the independence movement was often led by Scots Irish Protestants. Two hundred years ago, the English government promoted a quasi-religious association called the Orange Order whose purpose was to create bitterness and division between Protestants and native Irish Catholics. The English armed the Orange Order and sent them to kill and rampage in native villages. This had the intended effect of creating a deep chasm within Irish society that prevented any subsequent unified movement for independence.

These criminal seeds came to a bitter fruition in 1921, at the conclusion of the successful Irish rebellion. At that time the English forces rearmed the Orange Order, which immediately launched a pogrom to drive all native Irish out of Ulster, which was the region of the country that had a Scots Irish majority at the time. By the time the pogrom had run its course and Erin was partioned, the population of Ulster was 85 percent Scots Irish and 15 percent native Irish. Over the years, despite persecution, the native Irish population began gradually to overtake the Scots Irish population. By the late 1960s, the natives were about 30 percent of the population, and the handwriting was on the wall. If the trend was allowed to run its course, a day would come when the majority would be native Irish, and the demand for reunification with the Republic of Ireland would be irresistible. Faced with those conditions, a faction of the Orange Order undertook to repeat the pogrom and restore a safe Scots Irish majority in Ulster. At this time, the natives had found a defender, called the Irish Republican Army, which was a neighborhood defense militia. All the ingredients were in place for a renewal of the Civil War of 1921. As the troubles worsened, around 1970, the English government sent its troops to separate the warring factions.

The troops were initially welcomed, but rather quickly they were co-opted by the Orange Order, and simply added to the weight of forces arrayed against the native minority and its putative "army." At the same time, the military faction of the Orange Order continued in being and engaged in a long-running guerilla war with the I.R.A. Although the British forces had originally sided with the Scots Irish and the Orange Order, starting in the early 1980s the English adopted a more even-handed policy of trying to suppress both warring factions. The prisons were quickly filled with both Orange and native Irish fighters convicted of various kinds of attacks within Ulster and in England proper. The crimes for which they were sent to prison were often extremely serious: bombings that had had many casualties for instance, and attacks on the English government. But there were no executions for these crimes; all the convicts were consigned to prison.

As of today, nearly all of these prisoners have been released, regardless of what they were convicted of. The remarkable fact is the high degree of public support for their release, support that comes from both the native Irish and the Scots Irish communities. There is nearly universal agreement that the war is over and that it is time to forget and have peace. Implicit in this idea, by the way, is an acceptance of the Irish characterization of their men as not criminals but soldiers in a war for the rights of the native Irish community.

I do not hesitate to assert that this outcome of mutual reconciliation is better than anything that could have been achieved by sending these men to the gallows, even though I think that executions for murder would have been justified as a matter of a law. There are two factors at play in this case, however, that seem to be noteworthy at the least, and perhaps exceptional. They have to do with the fact that the Irish—native Irish and Scots Irish alike—are a soldier or warrior nation. One consideration is that it is unlikely that any number of executions would have deterred the native Irish. Much more likely, they would simply have made the conflict far bloodier than it already was. It may very well be impossible to deter a warrior nation from going to war. It is simply not something that they fear or want to avoid. At an individual level, everyone is sensitive to fear, but the culture and social organization of a warrior nation is designed specifically to overcome these individual feelings. Afghanistan seems a similar case.

There is a second consequence of a military culture. Among people for whom fighting is considered a rather normal, or at least inevitable, part of life, the warriors are taught not to take fighting personally: not to get their personal feelings entangled with their duties. Fighting is their duty or their occupation; they do not fight because they hate anyone, it is just a job.[5] As a result, when the war is over, it is over. There is no desire for revenge and no lingering animosity. Here again, the human person is always very inclined to seek revenge and to cherish old wounds. What is different in this case is that these feelings are not authenticated by the community. Quite the contrary, there is a consensus that it is time for peace, and that anyone who seeks revenge has violated the terms of his obligation to the community. This is a serious matter, because it was those terms that commissioned him with the moral authority to kill. Whoever seeks revenge is then by any standard a criminal against the society.

I neither recount these events nor I do not undertake this speculation about what they mean because I have a firm moral to draw. Just the opposite. I do not know what they mean or if they generalize in any way. The Irish are—despite their most cherished conceits—not unique, although there are not many truly warrior people. If there is a moral that seems to come from it, it is that in fixing punishments it is always necessary to look down the road to the eventual reconciliation of disputes, and in doing so it is always unwise to underestimate the capacity for healing and reconciliation.

Notes

1. See especially Isaac Ehrlich, "The Deterrent Effect of Capital Punishment—a Question of Life and Death," *American Economic Review* 65(3), (June, 1975). 397–517, Isaac Ehrlich, "Capital Punishment and Deterrence, Some Further Thoughts and Additional Evidence," *Journal of Political Economy* 85(4), (Aug. 1977): 741–788, Isaac Ehrlich and Joel Gibbons, "On the Measurement of the Deterrent Effect of Capital Punishment and the Theory of Deterrence," *Journal of Legal Studies.* 6(1) (January, 1977): 35–50, and Isaac Ehrlich and Zhi Qiang Liu, "Sensitivity Analyses of the Deterrence Hypothesis: Let's Keep the Econ in Econometrics," *Journal of Law and Economics* 62 (April 1999): 455–487. This line of research follows the theoretical argument of Gary Becker. See Gary S. Becker, "Crime and Punishment," *Journal of Political Economy* 76(2) (Mar.–Apr. 1968): 168–217.
2. One of the chief conclusions of Gary Becker—see the reference above—is that the easiest offenders to deter are those who are very sensitive to the risk of being arraigned and tried for a crime

because they fear any punishment at all. As a result, in any rational penal code, the threat of arraignment and trial will be at the margin the most effective deterrent.

3. I have emphasized the necessity of deterrence: that in many cases prevention or compensation are not feasible. Isaac Ehrlich and Gary Becker emphasize another consideration which introduces the psychology of the criminal. Most persons are risk averse, in the sense that when the future is uncertain they are particularly motivated by the extremely bad outcomes. Such persons are very susceptible to deterrence because making the punishment more severe is very effective, even when the punishment is rather unlikely to happen. They propose that the law would always want to raise the penalty for any crime to the point where no risk averse person would be willing to take such a chance. References to the theoretical work of Ehrlich and Becker are found in the papers cited above.

4. There is no clearer statement of this rule than the one found in the Roman Catechism of the Catholic Church. It reads, "There are some exceptions to the extent of this prohibition to killing. The power of life and death is permitted to certain civil magistrates because theirs is the responsibility under law to punish the guilt and protect the innocent. Far from being guilty of breaking this commandment, such an execution of justice is precisely an act of obedience to it. For the purpose of the law is to protect and foster human life. This purpose is fulfilled when the legitimate authority of the state is exercised by taking the guilty lives of those who have taken innocent life (The Fifth Commandment 4)."

5. A former mayor of Chicago and noted Irish American, Richard Daley, expressed this quite well when he advised his loyalists "Don't get mad. Get even." To get mad, in this sense, is to take the conflict and outcome personally, to get wrapped up in hatred and revenge. Then to get even, by contrast, is to keep the focus on winning and on accomplishing the result that the team is fighting for.

2

On Deterrence and Prevention

Blessed are they who hunger and thirst for justice,
for the kingdom of god will be theirs.

—Jesus of Nazareth

Civil society has many instruments at its disposal toward the goal of securing the peace, and the rights and freedoms of the citizens. Among them are punitive sanctions which are invoked under the umbrella of police powers. These sanctions fall into three broad categories: deterrence, incapacitation, and prevention. The law utilizes all three instruments, and they are not in any sense incompatible. They are however alternatives, and it is possible to substitute any one of them for any other. Many questions arise, both moral and pragmatic, but I will confine my attention in this essay to only one of them. Why do we rely on deterrence at all? Is it not inherently immoral? My conclusion, for which I will argue in this essay, is that deterrence is in truth both the *most* moral and the most effective of sanctions. While society must use all the available tools to some extent, deterrence should always be preferred wherever possible.

This is as good a place as any to make the definitions of the three terms explicit. Deterrence is a sanction that makes an example of one person with the intent to discourage others from committing the same crime. Incapacitation is simply preventing a convicted criminal from repeating his offense. Prevention is preventing persons in general from undertaking a particular course of action, which includes preventing them from committing a particular crime. An example makes these concepts clear.

Consider how they apply to rape and murder carried out late at night in public places. It is an application of deterrence to impose a very harsh prison term on someone convicted of this crime, to the extent that other persons will avoid this crime for fear of ending up in the same way. The prison term is itself an example of incapacitation, at least for the length of the term. Prevention is rather different, and comes in two forms. Passive prevention consists of measures like lighting dark areas and patrolling regularly. Active prevention consists of some intervention in the lives of the general public, such as a curfew. Prevention and deterrence have in common that they are directed not to known criminals but to unidentified, potential ones. For the most part, passive preventives are almost never controversial and have understandably the highest degree of public support. Wherever in this essay I use them term "prevention," understand that I have in mind active prevention.

Before we go on, there is another aspect of this example that merits some attention. I took as an example of a crime the act of "rape and murder carried out late at night in public places." That is not a moral definition of the crime, because in a moral sense it makes no difference when or where the rape and murder occurred. But they are part of the legal definition of the crime, and these qualifiers have both practical and moral implications. The issue that the law must deal with is not one of who is a nice person and who is not such a nice person. The concern of the law is what is going on out there is the world and what to do about it. The definition of the crime therefore has to indicate at least in a rough way what sort of preventive measures might be taken.

More importantly, it must also specify in a rough way factors that bear on the seriousness of the crime. In general, kinds of crimes that occur rarely are inherently less serious than commonplace ones because the public is far more threatened, and the confidence of the public in the law more deeply shaken. It is for this reason that the law freely takes into account so-called "exonerating circumstances," which are in fact just parts of the definition of the crime at hand that make it less serious than most crimes from the broader category it represents.

The practical consequences of this difference are of course readily apparent. The moral side of it may not be immediately obvious. The moral issues that the criminal law raises are not those of personal morality. The community is not the moral judge of the offender. Only the Lord god judges the person. The morality that is at issue has to do with the conduct of the law, and especially whether its methods are appropriate to its purposes.[1] The moral law requires that equal offenses be treated equally, and it also requires that the minimum sanction be used. We express this when we say that the punishment ought to fit the crime. What we mean is that it should not be needlessly exacting. Put differently, the sanction—whatever it is—should be chosen to serve the rational purposes of the law and not to appease a desire for revenge. This rule applies of course between broad categories of crimes, e.g. the punishment for car theft should be less than that for murder. It applies also between different forms of a given offense. Thus for instance, crimes committed by persons who abuse a position of trust are always more serious than are the same crimes between unrelated persons. The seriousness of the crime depends upon all its circumstances, and on how they threaten the civil order and the confidence and safety of the public.

To summarize, the law has at its disposal three methods of defending the public order and the rights of the citizens—deterrence, incapacitation, and prevention—and in practice it uses a combination of all three. In this short essay I will consider each of them in turn, but I will start with incapacitation. It is unlike the others in that they are directed chiefly at influencing the actions of third parties, while incapacitation targets the offender alone.

Incapacitation and the Law

Incapacitation raises in the most direct way possible questions about the degree of harshness of sanctions. For this reason conflicts can arise between incapacitation and deterrence, when it seems that the goal of deterrence calls for harsher treatment of the individual than his particular circumstances would seem to warrant or justify.

While in the particular, it often seems as though deterrence can call for more drastic sanctions than we would want to mete out to a particular offender, from a broader perspective deterrence serves to moderate incapacitation. The logic of this is actually transparent. If we were to lose hope of achieving deterrence, incapacitation and prevention would be the only remaining ways of controlling criminal behavior and of defending the civil order. Offenders would have to be incapacitated for much longer terms or in more stringent ways than we do in fact use. The case of murder provides a telling example. Because potential criminals do in fact respond to the threat of punishment, a relatively few executions for murder prevents many. Without deterrence, it would be necessary either to execute many more hardened criminals, or to lock them away for life. The effectiveness of deterrence and of prevention thus serves to greatly reduce the need for incapacitation.

In fact, no criminal justice system could possibly survive if it were predicated solely on incapacitation. The sheer cost of all aspects of the legal process and of the penalties would be overwhelming. The cost of police, courts, and prisons is sometimes invoked in discussion of criminal justice, but usually it arises with a sense of embarrassment, as though it is somehow unseemly to mix money and the law. It is very true that not all dollars are alike in this matter. The cost of criminality is a cost imposed on the individual, while the cost of law enforcement is one that he expressly assents to. This is an enormous difference precisely because the end of the law is to preserve the freedoms of the person to govern his own life. It may be said that the two costs come in somewhat different denominations. But it is also true that after we make the necessary conversion between currencies, cost is, in the end, cost. It does little good to create a judicial monstrosity that consumes the wealth of the community in order to stop the members from stealing from each other. We tolerate, as we must eventually tolerate, some level of criminality because the cost to reduce it further simply could not be justified, and this is especially apt in the matter of incapacitation because that approach is so very expensive.

In this regard I would propose that in America today we actually rely excessively on incapacitation, and that, more to the point, our prison terms are too long. I propose this point purely in my capacity as a citizen, and not as in any way a matter of law. The reasoning that leads me to this conclusion, however, is compelling. Our existing sentencing rules have brought us an ever expanding prison population, and a public expense that grows even faster than that. The proposition does not actually rest only on cost, however. It rests on noting how punitive long terms of imprisonment really are. We almost casually lock men and women—but nearly all men in practice—away for terms of many years. In some cases, the term is for life without parole. I describe our attitude as being almost casual, because in practice the convicts are invisible to us. They are marched off to the cells and never return to absorb our attention or to haunt our conscience. They simply disappear. This blindness is one of the most pressing and contentious moral issues that the criminal law raises.

What I propose is that the law adopt a single maximum term of prison that applies to each person. To make this point more precise, let's say we fix it at twelve years. Then this is the law: no person can be made to spend more than twelve years of his life in prison. Period. I do not mean on a per offense basis. I mean total. The prisons cannot take more than a dozen years from any person over the course of his life. Twelve years in penitentiary is an enormous time. We casually assign longer terms only because we are blind to what they actually mean for the person. A dozen years from the adult life of a person is, in many respects his whole life. What years are left to him after that can at best serve him to put his life together again in some limited way. He emerges without family, without job or career, and without having exercised much freedom as an adult. He will at best survive for what remains of his life, unless he is a person not only of great character, but of great good luck also. It is simply wrong and indefensible to incapacitate anyone for more than some number like a dozen years. Life in prison *is* taking life, but taking it on the installment plan.

Two courses of action, or perhaps two lines of reasoning, apply to persons for whom a dozen years does not seem like enough. One case would be the compulsive pickpocket who had already served six terms of two years each. What do we do when he is arrested for the seventh time? What I propose is that we say we did our best. Since there will always be pickpockets, he will, it seems, always be one of them. The nation will survive. If he was first convicted at eighteen years of age, something like twenty years have now elapsed, counting his dozen years in penitentiary, and he is thirty-eight. He will soon be too slow for that game anyway, and will have to get honest by default. I do not of course rule out a sincere effort to guide him to a better way of life in society. These efforts should begin in prison, but will probably have to be continued thereafter too.

The other course, for the most exceptional cases, is execution. If there is a person whose crimes are simply intolerable to society, and for whom even twelve years in penitentiary were not a sufficient deterrent, more years are not promising. We can hardly have the right to take his life one day at a time unless we also can claim the right to put him to death. If, moreover, even a dozen years in penitentiary were not sufficient to cause him to acknowledge his guilt and to reform his life, there is only one last chance for him. Perhaps the fear of the rope can accomplish what a cozy cell could not.

Since I began this section on incapacitation with a note about the expense involved, the reader may leap at this point to the conclusion that I want to use execution as a cost-saving measure. That is by no means true. What prompts this proposal is a recognition of the inhumanity of unlimited prison terms, and of the ease with which the public blinds itself to the plight of those in penitentiary. We do not understand how terrible it is because we do not want to know, and because it all takes place in "there," hidden from view. Am I then proposing that the convicts would perhaps rather be dead? No, I am not asserting that either. These are measures for persons whom we do not ever want to deal with or allow into our society again. If that is a judgement we are willing to make then we cannot delude ourselves that we are not taking life just because we take it one day at a time.

It is actually not clear whether adopting a maximum term of prison would save money or would cost money. If we did this in a way that greatly increased the crime rate, we would be imprisoning more persons. More persons but fewer years per person. . . . The net result is problematical. It goes without saying that I do not want this conundrum to arise, and that the term limit should be accompanied by other measures that would prevent such a counterproductive outcome.

The Moral Authority to Punish

Many persons of good will question today whether it is advisable for the state to execute any person. That is an open question, and one that the public has to decide for themselves. It is moreover not a matter that can be decided once and for all because it depends on the circumstances that the community finds itself in and the kinds of grave crimes that it must deal with. Other persons question whether the state has the right to execute. This is moral myopia. I have emphasized that execution and imprisonment are morally equivalent. Whether we take the convict's life, part of his life, or his whole life one day at a time are exactly equivalent. Indeed, they are morally equivalent to fines. Execution is not murder, but if it was murder, then imprisonment would equally be slavery and fines would be theft.

Imprisonment as Deterrent

The length and severity of prison terms figures in both incapacitation and deterrence. One very plausible objection to what I propose is that it diminishes the deterrent threat of prison. While that is strictly true it needs to be placed in perspective. First of all, as I noted previously, persons who are not deterred by the threat of so many years in prison—whether that number is twelve years or somewhat more—are not likely to be more intimidated by the threat of an even longer term. There simply has to be diminishing returns. We must in any case weigh this effect against the injury done to persons who should be released much earlier. It is possible that incapacitation can be reconciled with a desire to minimize punishment by judgmental programs for early release on parole.

A Further Note on Imprisonment

One matter that always arises in regard to prison terms is whether convicts should be put to work as part of their sentence. The most obvious point, and the one that should be made first, is that purposeful labor is inherently good for the person. For that reason alone it is good for prisoners to work. Since criminals very often have little to offer in terms of job skills and attainments, their work in prison also affords an opportunity to gain essential job training. Not only is this a great benefit to the convict, it is also invaluable for the prison because it keeps the inmates engaged at tasks that are highly rewarding and at the same time instills hope for the future. All of this is just common sense, and is of course universally practiced in penitentiaries all over the world.

While it is essential for everyone involved that the convicts work, it is equally essential that they be paid an approximately market wage for the work they do. It may seem at first glance as though the convicts would be thankful just to have work, and that it is not necessary to pay them very much. That is true as far as it goes, but it leaves a very dangerous distortion in place. It may well be true that the convicts could be forced to work for little or no wages, and that they might actually be better off than if they had to work at all. The problem with using them as slave labor is not what it does to the convicts, but what it does to the law. It creates an incentive to create spurious offenses for the sole aim of sending persons to prison. The English penal—which is to say slave labor—colonies make this point. English rule in Erin included laws against, for instance, wearing a mustache, speaking the Irish language, teaching an Irish child to read or write. All of these crimes were punishable by exportation to the prison colonies. It seems on the face of it highly doubtful that the King or Parliament actually cared whether Irish men wore mustaches or long braids. It is far more likely that they were fond of the cheap pressed labor in their fledgling colonies. The poor people of England fared very little better, though the exact list of crimes was of course different. In more recent times under the totalitarian regimes in Russia legions of persons were shipped off to work in Siberia on various pretexts. This particular form of corruption of the law has appeared in many times and places, which is all the more reason that it is necessary to expressly and vigorously oppose it.

These remarks are all I have to say about incapacitation itself. Next I will turn to the other two instruments, but I will take them together because the most pressing issue is what they have in common: that they are ways to influence the actions of unknown persons.

Deterrence and Prevention and the Law

> The purpose of locks is to keep honest persons honest.
>
> —Attributed to Confucius

Incapacitation alone cannot possibly accomplish by itself the maintaining of civil order. It is simply too costly in every sense of the term to impose harsh enough sanctions against enough criminals to preserve order and civil rights. I have just argued that in fact at the present time we rely too heavily on incapacitation, at least to the extent that our prison terms are excessive. The law cannot in fact do its job without relying primarily on keeping honest persons honest. The alternative is just too destructive.

In the end the limiting factor on the severity of punishments is that they call into question the legitimacy of the law itself. The public cannot help but recognize eventually that they have a choice between the criminals and the cops. If the cops become too great a threat to human rights and freedoms, a prudent public will reason that they are better off to take their chances with the criminals. This choice does not arise except in the most extreme circumstances, such as under a regime imposed on the community by a foreign conqueror, but it is a needed reminder that the legitimacy of the public authorities is not in the final analysis an absolute. It is no mere illusion that the public often sides sympathetically with the defense in criminal trials, nor is it necessarily a mistake to do so even when the defendant seems clearly to be guilty.

Deterrence and prevention substitute for incapacitation and also substitute for each other. They are, however, not at all the same thing. As defined previously, deterrence works by making an example of the convicted criminal. It is defined and carried out with the legal and penal system. Prevention works by imposing restrictions directly on the public. Thus there are differences according to who and which institutions are responsible, and there are differences of practical effect.

Apart from these factors, the difference between deterrence and prevention has a deeply moral dimension as well. The cornerstone of all human rights and freedoms is the conviction that we are moral agents, empowered with reason, memory, and free will. Our reason is far from perfect. Our memory is perhaps at times even more problematical. Our wills are never in this world entirely free. The fact remains, however, that we have these faculties as a birthright on account of our human nature. All human rights and freedoms belong to us because our human nature enables us, on the one hand, to use them, and because they are necessary for the fulfillment of our calling. We have both the capacity to use these fundamental freedoms and the need and the duty to use them.[2] The civil order exists precisely to promote our human rights and freedoms, and it would be paradoxical in the extreme if the exactions of the law were actually to deny them to the citizens. No demand upon the law is therefore more fundamental than that it engage the person as a moral agent, not defeating, but rather utilizing, his or her mind and will to promote the civil order.

It may at first blush seem as if this maxim contradicts the punitive aspect of the law itself. How can it be reconciled with long prison terms and exhausting fines? The answer is of course that while we as human beings are moral agents, we do not always act morally. Our reason is faulty, our memory selective, and our will perverse at times. The law exists for those times when the moral agent acts in immoral ways.

These remarks serve as a starting point to rethink the application of prevention, and to contrast it with deterrence. The goal, stated with perhaps over-simple directness, of prevention is to stop the exercise of free will on the part of the general public. It has in common with incapacitation that it acts directly to control actions. This contrasts with deterrence, which relies on the intimidating example of punishment. Deterrence, whatever else maybe said about it, has the virtue that it fully engages the moral person. It simply makes the outcomes of choices more stark and forces, or seeks to force, each citizen to think carefully about what he or she is doing. Prevention by contrast takes away the power to choose.

The Case of "Gun Control"

No example makes these issues clearer than the ongoing debate over so-called "gun control." I take that to mean laws that to some extent or other make it impossible for the general citizens to possess guns and ammunition. Certainly the innumerable particular bills that have been proposed in the name of gun control almost all have much more modest pretensions. They generally are written to make it just a little more difficult to own a gun, rather than to make it impossible. This difference of degrees raises an important point which is quite apart from the matter of gun control as prevention, and so I will deal with it first. The law, as with everything else in life, entirely comfortable with differences of degree. But the differences contemplated here are not of that sort. The only real difference of substance between the little pecks at gun control, the little nods in the general direction of gun control, that surface from time to time, and outright confiscation of guns is that they are ineffectual and misdirected by design. Put in its starkest terms, for rhetorical purposes, the situation is like this. We have a certain population of really dangerous persons who have guns. Our fraudulent nod at gun control is then comparable to asking the rest of the public—the really dangerous persons do not care a whit what rules we make and so they are necessarily exempt from them—to please leave their guns at home on Tuesdays. The presumed defense for this nonsense, the justification that its proponents offer, is that it will be entirely ineffectual and will in reality do nothing whatever. The persons who care what the rules say were not actually carrying guns around to shoot each other anyway, and even if they were, they would be just as content to do the killing on Wednesday. The point, of course, is that a self-defeating law and an effective law do not differ in degree. They differ in intent. The endless rhetoric of gun control is just a sort of sad shadow theater offered to appease persons who are genuinely frightened by the abundance of guns in the community, without actually changing anything.

It was highly revealing that following the terrible shootings at Columbine High School the usual chorus of gun control was raised in earnest, and that it continued until cooler heads pointed out that the two killers had violated something like seventeen of the more than two thousand "controls" already on the books. It is pretty hard to miss the fact that simply adding more pages to the federal code is, in this matter, being treated not a means to an end, but is actually the end itself. We can safely infer from this history that practically no one is actually proposing to control guns.

Deterrence

Since prevention seems not to be an option, is there a way to deter armed crimes? The preceding recitation does not vitiate the case for actual gun control, and despite the examples cited, gun control can be done in degrees. It is not an all-or-noting proposition. Yet prevention would have to be recognized as insufficient. To generalize, the community weighs the merits of prevention against those of deterrence as it forges a comprehensive plan to stop all sorts of crimes before they happen, and in weighing them it judges the degrees of each to apply. Just as deterrence and prevention permit the law to cut back on incapacitation—to fix lesser penalties to convicts—so also do they substitute for each other. This is good in itself, and accordingly the both tactics should be used. In weighing them, the community has to take account of both the practical and the moral implications of each, and both the practical and the moral outcomes of its decisions. I have defined deterrence as making an example of the convict in order to impress other persons. The practical issue is whether deterrence actually works. The research by Prof. Isaac Ehrlich among others contains very compelling evidence that it does though I will not stop here to review the evidence. Deterrence works.

The proposition that deterrence works should in fact be a cornerstone of the criminal law. I have written elsewhere that deterrence is the morality—the moral rationale—for punishment. The purpose of the criminal law is to preserve human rights and freedoms. In totalitarian society, the purpose is presumably to ensure that no one bothers the sovereign and in feudal society the law defends the rights and privileges of the aristocracy. We, however, are making laws for all the people, and the only possible rationale is therefore justice. But what can be said of a people who are immune to deterrence? They would be so lacking in reason or in self-control—which is a precondition for freedom—that they would have no rights and freedoms to defend. Persons who are immune to deterrents are simply to that degree not moral agents. They do not surrender their humanity, and for such persons—the mentally handicapped, the young, and the irrational—society takes extraordinary measures to preserve their human dignity. But such persons have limited capacity to make moral judgements. If we assume that all of the citizens are in that state, that none of the citizens is truly a moral agent, then there is simply nothing left to defend. Government and law would not be a matter of serving the public, they would be more in the nature of herding the cattle. If deterrents do not actually deter, we would have at the same time no practical reason to invoke them and no justification either.

The clearest deterrent to using guns to carry out other crimes is simply to heighten the punishment in these cases, and this of course is already done. Armed robbery is more than robbery; assault with a deadly weapon is more than assault by itself. I am not aware of systematic research to identify and quantify the effectiveness of these incremental sanctions, but it deserves to be studied. Lacking the research, we are confined to qualitative propositions.

It does not vitiate this argument at all that there are occasions where deterrence does not work. In times of war the soldiers knowingly and willingly expose themselves to dangers that would under any ordinary circumstance deter any reasoning person. Deterrence is not perfect, and it is not designed to be perfect. It is designed to raise the stakes involved in breaking the law. Some persons will be deterred and others will not. The deterrent is incremental and partial, but it is nonetheless valuable and legitimate.

Since deterrence is, to repeat my phrase from above, the morality of punishment, it is questionable whether the law can apply sanctions in cases where there can be no deterrent. We already recognize this in the case of the "insane." The insane, for this purpose, are those persons who are not susceptible to deterrents, and who are simply unable to respond to the threat of deterrence. It serves no purpose in a practical sense to punish them because it does not promote the goal of deterrence to do so. This point was first made by Prof. Gary Becker, whose seminal work on criminal law has been the inspiration for many other persons and was recognized by the Nobel committee in awarding him his laurels in economics.[3] We observe, by the way, that in this case the capacity of the offender becomes in effect part of the definition of the crime: theft by an insane person is actually a different crime from theft by a rational person. Different not because of the practical or moral effect of the theft—the effect on the victim—but different because it demands different actions from the community which must manage its crime problem. The criminal law is not a law for judging what people do; it is a vehicle for defending human rights and the civil order. Its morality is calibrated by how and how well it does that. The fact that some crimes are immune to deterrence is always a reason for preventive steps.

Prevention

Prevention is in important ways the very opposite of deterrence, and where they differ the contrast is generally unfavorable to prevention. Deterrence engages the will and reason of the citizen by confronting him with tough choices. As a result, fewer of the citizens choose to engage in criminal activity. Prevention by contrast supplants the will and reason of the individual citizen. The implication is that prevention is not inherently a moral instrument. It is by contrast inherently immoral. Prevention is sometimes however more practically effective than deterrence, and it can be justified on grounds of effectiveness.

Why is prevention inherently immoral? That is very easy to explain. By supplanting the freedom of the citizens, it thwarts the precise end that the law is intended to promote. Prevention treats all the citizens as suspects, if not as outright criminals. The example of gun control is again a good case in point. There are many ways to actually disarm the citizens. In practice they would be impossibly difficult to implement, and I will return to that point in a moment, but for the moment I am satisfied that there are at least in theory—on paper—actual ways to round up all the firearms. Why don't we do that? Quite simply, it is because to do so would demand that we treat every citizen like a prisoner. The authors of the American Constitution had a very good reason for ensuring that the citizens would have the right to possess weapons. They reasoned that citizens of a free country must have that right. How indeed can we justify letting the citizens choose our president, who commands our entire nuclear arsenal, if we cannot trust them to own guns? People who cannot be trusted with guns certainly cannot be trusted to vote for their leaders who wield vastly more firepower than the common citizens do. In a democracy it is simply not permitted to treat the citizens like the enemy or like criminals. No democracy could survive for any length of time on that basis.

One of the very most disturbing things about the seemingly incessant clamor for so-called "gun control" is that no one seems to step forward to make this rather fundamental and self-evident observation. It seems to be accepted without question that gun control is a moral imperative, while in fact it is the height of both illogic and immorality. It stems not from a moral sense, but from raw fear of one's neighbors, a fear so vivid that it comprehends treating them like an enemy. Such a community is headed for civil war. Then the guns will be abundant and loud.

The justification for prevention has to be practical rather than moral, to repeat an earlier remark. One may ask how that is possible. How can we justify measures of suspect morality on the grounds that they are effective? The answer is that in any actual community in this world, while we establish civil order to promote and defend freedom, freedom is never perfect. Tradeoffs arise naturally when we set out to maximize personal freedom and to ensure human rights. Everyone will happily sacrifice a little freedom to the civil authorities, who are in any case answerable to the citizens, in order not to lose a great deal of freedom to the criminals.

The fact that the civil authorities are accountable to the public is an important consideration, because prevention is so inherently dangerous. One of the gravest dangers that it raises is potentially to undermine the public confidence in these authorities' control. Whenever the government imposes some preventive measure on the community, any citizens who did not buy into the decision at the outset then also question whether their interests are being protected. They question whether the authorities have assumed powers that undermine the very accountability that is a necessary precondition for limiting the freedoms of the citizens. There is bound to be a wide range of opinion in every case, and some persons are by nature so suspicious of the law and of the governors that even the slightest imposition on them in perceived as tyranny. Other citizens, by contrast, are so docile that the very question seemingly never arises. Every healthy community deals daily with just this sort of issue every day, and such conflicts are inevitable. It is well, however, to be conscious of the dangers that follow from too vigorous an application of prevention.

I will return one last time to the topic of gun control, to make the point that since the justification for prevention is a pragmatic one, questions of effectiveness are of paramount importance. Ineffective, or even more so counterproductive, preventive measures cannot be justified in any way. I asserted above that true gun control is in theory possible, but this theory is not reality. Two contrary facts intervene between them. First of all is the observation that if it is illegal to sell a gun, only criminals will sell guns. If the public still wants to have guns, they will have to fatten the wallets of the criminal organizations to get them. This would give the criminals a monopoly so valuable that even the dollar value of the drug monopoly fades into insignificance. The criminals moreover have a means at hand to make possessing a gun not only desirable but essential. If in any particular neighborhood there are initially no guns in circulation there will be little demand for a gun on the part of the ordinary citizens. A gun-free community is potentially a stable, self-sustaining equilibrium. But not when the gun-dealing gangs show up. They have the capacity to make everyone a gun owner, and if they are the only provider of guns, they have every incentive to do so. Initially the police will oppose them vigorously, but time is not on the side of the police. All the gangs need to do is to jeopardize the civil order by provoking attacks here and there to create the demand. It is impossible that the police could be so effective as to prevent almost every outbreak of crime or violence.

This is not the only limit to the potential effectiveness of this attempt at prevention. There is another possible tactic of gun control, which would be to attack not the sellers of guns, but the manufacturers. The approach shows some promise at first blush, because while there are potentially many sellers, there are only a few manufacturers. While true as it applies to the world today, this statement begs an important point about gun manufacture. There are only a few today because the industry is competitive and only firms with economies of scale can survive. There is in principle no limit, however, to the potential number of gun makers. The technology is by no means arcane. The original Colt revolver, made in 1844, is still a very effective weapon today. There are undoubtedly thousands of machine shops in America that could make them. All that is needed is the steel, and surely there is no way that we can make steel a controlled substance. The ammunition is also easy to manufacture, and the technology of propellants, of chemical explosives, is again very widely known. The point of this recitation is of course that there is not going to be in reality any gun control. That is simply out of the question regardless of how determined the authorities might be to achieve it. The drastic steps they would have to take, if they were really committed to gun control, would have to rapidly exhaust the public acceptance of the effort and in the end undermine their own legitimacy.

It is always easy to put together an argument, like the one above, for inaction. This one happens to be completely compelling, but even then it leaves open the question of what we should as a community do. If we cannot prevent—except for egregious cases—persons from getting guns, should we just surrender?

Obviously I do not think so. There would be no point in writing an essay on the law and the defense of civil order if in the end I plan to give up in despair. Some preventive measures are effective and justified. Do them certainly. But more to the point, this is an area where it is absolutely essential to rely on deterrence. Anyone can steal your purse. If the thief is caught, he goes to jail for a year. Anyone can commit armed robbery too, but if that person is caught the result is a lot more time in prison. We as a community wish that we could never have to worry about robbery or armed robbery, but here in this world that is not possible. Deterrence is the way to ensure at least that they are as infrequent as possible.

Modern Police Methods

In the last decade there has been a significant change in police methods, emphasizing a more visible and more active police presence on the streets. The resulting reduction in crime of all kinds has been very gratifying. The bedrock of the new method has been to put more police out where the people are and to react to smaller misdemeanors.

To some degree the change represents an application of prevention, but in reality it is a kind of deterrence. As I mentioned previously, the empirical studies of crime and deterrents show, as predicted by Gary Becker, that crime rates are most susceptible to the risk of arrest and arraignment.[4] When a police patrol is on the scene, the probability of apprehension is high. Even the most foolhardy risk takers find that crime is unrewarding when there is little chance of success. Raising the certainty of arrest—thwarting the criminal undertaking directly—is the most effective way to deter. This is actually, of course, a return to much older police methods. The word police itself implies a presence on the street. Policing went through a phase in which rapid response of police was thought to replace the patrol. This was the period of "high tech," capital-intensive policing. Since the street riots in Los Angeles however the rapid response regime has been discredited, and patrolling is back.

The preventive effect of more aggressive patrolling obviously can not be discounted, but no matter how many police are on the street, they are most unlikely to be at exactly the right place, at the right time. That would simply be too expensive. Patrol is very expensive because police are highly trained and highly paid these days, and that naturally limits its use. But a compromise solution, which involves keeping police close enough to the scene so that they can respond almost immediately is feasible and has been very effective.

Along with the return to a regime of police presence, police methods have also changed to implement more intimidation in their dealings with the citizens. Everyone has read stories of elderly grandmothers being led off to jail in handcuffs, and grade school children being hit with powerful tazers. This is obviously abusive police work, and it can only serve to undermine the legitimacy of the police. These practices paint the police as the enemy. They are bad police work and they are a violation of precisely that which the law is intended to secure. It makes little difference to me to be attacked and disabled by men in police uniforms or men in ski masks. If there is good reason for that treatment—if I am an immediate danger to persons near me—no one will sympathize with my plight. If however, it is clearly unnecessary force, the public is liable to side with me and to ask what separates the police from the criminals.

The community simply does not want police who overreact. This is a similar situation to the one where legitimate doubt exists about whether the legal process is able to convict the guilty and acquit the innocent. The answer is of course to not give up. The answer is to get better police. In point of fact, police today are quite well trained and are for the most part very well able to do their job right. They need to operate under rules and policies that reinforce that. Persons who cannot do their jobs without resorting to excessive force do not belong in uniform. The premise of the police patrol is, after all, not that the police can and will track down and kill fleeing suspects. That is not necessary in all but the most drastic cases. The presence of police is principally to make it clear to the offender that he has been seen and consequently that he will not get away. We should be reminded here of how many years the British police did not even carry firearms.

Prevention and Natural Deterrents

Liberty is not a means to a higher political end.
It is itself the highest political end.

—Lord Acton

Both prevention and deterrence arise in contexts other than the criminal code and law enforcement. While in many ways therefore the essential issues are different, there is a common element that merits attention here because it brings into focus again key issues of rights and of morality. Stripped to its basics, deterrence is the capacity of reasoning persons to take into account remote, contingent results of their decisions and of their actions. Anything that can produce painful results is therefore a kind of deterrent. The proverbial hot stove is one such natural deterrent. More to the point here, however, are natural deterrents that have gotten dragged into the tort law, and have gotten entangled in the doctrine of strict liability.

There are many examples, but railway crossings are a good place to start. The obvious disadvantages of being hit by a freight train are an unmistakable example of a natural deterrent, and reasoning persons who wish to live make it a point not to cross in front of fast moving trains. One could hardly argue that any sort of active prevention would be needed to stop the citizen from dying on the railway right-of-way. Amazingly, the law seems to adopt this most improbable premise.

The tort law—which is a companion of the criminal

code dealing with private remedies for wrongs against the person—has adopted a rule of absolute liability on the part of the railroad, which requires that the carrier indemnify the survivors of an accident. Thus the company is required to provide a kind of accidental death insurance to survivors of persons who die on its tracks. This rule provides a motive to suicide on the tracks that can cause a person who is sufficiently desperate to provide for his family to take his own life. The rationale for this rule of law is that the deceased cannot be held accountable for his own actions—the possibility of intentional suicide is simply ruled out by assumption—and that the railroad company is in some way partially responsible, or perhaps entirely responsible, for the accident. The company actually has in practice no possible defense because its tort is that the deceased is dead, and that is unquestionably true. The law of absolute liability in cases like this shifts responsibility away from the person, who is in a position to exercise judgment and self-control, and toward an entity that cannot.

Since there are in fact many fatalities each year on every railroad right-of-way, the cost to the railroads of providing this sort of death benefit free of charge is very high. The railroad companies are not slow to appeal to the responsible governments—usually the towns and the states—to limit their potential liability. There are many passive preventives like crossbars and warning lights that are not controversial, but these have proved to be insufficient. More direct measures are being adopted which include police patrols at busy railroad crossings and onerous fines levied on persons who cross when they are not supposed to. We no longer trust rational persons to cross the tracks when it is safe for them. We try to substitute the governance of the police for the intelligence of the citizens. The person is then treated like a recalcitrant child, in need of guidance from the law and the police and liable for rather costly fines if he rejects this treatment. The illogic of this proposition is transparently clear: why would a suicidal person care what the police want him to do and why would a prudent person need them? It would be far better to bear in mind that bit of nineteenth century wisdom cited at the start of this part: "If the law supposes that, the Law is a ass, a idiot."[5]

This example, by no means unique, poses in very clear terms the inherent contradiction between prevention and the central premise of civil society, which is to preserve the rights and freedoms of moral agents. Persons who need to be prevented from stepping in front of fast freights are simply not in practice moral agents. From a purely logical perspective, though not one that I endorse of course, this supposes that citizens in general do not in fact have—they are incapable of having—any rights and freedoms to defend. As I noted previously, I recognize that some persons—the young for instance—do in some degree lack these capacities. But they are not representative of the public as a whole. It is they who are in special circumstances, and whom we care for especially because of our commitment to their essential human dignity.

Conclusion

The criminal law is a highly complex entity that uses the tactics at its disposal to preserve human rights and freedoms in an imperfect world. It is a fact of life that the tools of the law are themselves a threat, or can be a threat, to the very rights they are intended to preserve. It is also true that even the perception of power that they confer on the leaders of society is deemed sometimes to be a threat, and provokes a violent reaction among a mistrustful population. The ordinary citizen confers on the law enormous legitimacy and authority even while reserving to himself deep misgivings about how that power is being applied.

In this setting it is essential first of all for the authorities to use every available tactic in order no to come to rely too heavily on any single one of them. The goal is to use many approaches in order to manage the incidence of crime. It is not the goal to reduce the rate to zero. It is better to endure some level of crime than to attempt to stop it altogether, recognizing that nothing in the world is perfect. This of course is what communities actually do. There is no place that is free of crime, and no place were the public would endure for even a day the extreme exertions that would be needed to stop all crime.

It is also highly desirable that the tactic used be as consonant as possible with the goals of the law. This, as I have argued above, implies that we should tilt toward deterrence and away from active prevention. It implies also that except for the death penalty, which is an exceptional case, we should limit the size of sanctions so that they not effectively take the life of the criminal under the guise of fines or prison.

Notes

1. I do not mean in any way to deny that the moral sense of the public is rightly engaged in formulating the criminal code, and that matters of human rights and freedoms, which the law serves to defend, are inherently moral. There can indeed be no justice that defies the moral law. The public does not have the right to act ar-

bitrarily or without regard to personal rights in the course of pre-serving those same rights, but makes them the centerpiece of the law. Personal morality is an integral part of human rights and freedoms too. For the purposes of this essay, however, I take the content of the actual laws as a given, and focus here only on how to manage the legal process itself.

2. The recognition of the moral nature of human rights is fully rec-ognized in our Declaration of Independence, which posits that we have inalienable human rights: rights that are an integral part of our human nature and that cannot be lost or removed. We have these rights as an inalienable gift because, in parallel fash-ion, we have the capacity to use them.

3. See: Gary S. Becker "Crime and Punishment: An Economic Ap-proach," *Journal of Political Economy* 76 (1967): 169–217. Pro-fessor Becker's study of crime and deterrence has yielded many valuable insights. Among them is the observation that the civil authorities control two companion factors, the Magnitude of sanctions and the Probability of being caught and punished. Some persons are most sensitive to the magnitude, and for them deterrence is highly effective. Even if heavy sanctions are rarely applied, the sheer weight of them deters risk-averse persons. Risk-taking persons are, by contrast, more sensitive to the prob-ability of being caught and punished, because other things being equal they are willing to take their chances of escaping punish-ment altogether. Such persons are not very susceptible to deter-rents. Professor Becker continues then by observing that since the cost to the community of imposing sanctions is roughly equal to the product of the magnitude and the probability, we should always learn toward infrequent, harsh penalties. This has the ef-fect of deterring, at relatively small cost, the risk-averse mem-bers of the society.

4. Besides the articles cited previously, see Isaac Ehrlich, "Partici-pation in Illegitimate Activities: A Theoretical and Empirical In-vestigation," *Journal of Political Economy* 81 (97): 521.

5. This saying is attributed to Mr. Bumble, speaking in Charles Dickens's *Oliver Twist*.

3

Penal Options for Dealing with Grave and Heinous Crime: Another Way

For more than two hundred years the option to execute those who commit serious and heinous crimes has been attacked and defended by many able thinkers and from many different perspectives. The main course of history has been for this option to lose favor steadily. At the present time most of the Western world has decided that it will not execute criminals for any reason, and the public outcry from that quarter is shrill and uncompromising. The Catholic Church has weighed into the debate, taking a somewhat lonely middle path. This is moreover far from being the first wave of abolitionist fervor in history. Under the circumstances this may be a good time to rethink what execution means, why it should or should not be invoked, and indeed how society should deal with grave crime. Contrary to the almost messianic fervor of the abolitionists, this is not an either/or issue pitting us against them. When demands are raised in uncompromising terms, as they are in this matter, the only certainty is that the real issues have been forgotten by people who see it is a simple test of wills and who can accept nothing less than to get their way.

This essay follows on and expands on some thoughts that I first enunciated in the preceding chapters. In order not to waste the valuable time of those whose minds are closed on this subject, I will say at the start that I am convinced that execution of criminals is a necessary and appropriate punishment under certain circumstances. What those circumstances are and how they fit into the overall framework of criminal penalties are the topic of this essay.

Crime and Human Rights

The criminal and penal law is just one facet of a structure of social control by which a community or nation, acting through their governments and their courts of law, recognize and defend human rights. In the discussion that follows, it may seem in places that I neglect or even discard the moral and ethical aspects of criminal law and criminal sanctions. That is very far from the case. The community and their government are bound to and bound by the grant of human rights that is the birthright of every person. Indeed, the law exists only to confirm and to implement these rights which, to paraphrase Thomas Jefferson, cannot be lost or taken away by any mortal law or civil authority. They are part of the constitution of human beings and our birthright from the Lord god who fashioned us. This is not a controversial proposition, nor is it questioned by either party to this debate. All accept the legitimacy of courts and laws and punishments, and this is true even of those who do not accept Jefferson's words or any debt to their creator.

The context of this issue is therefore one of method as well as of implementation. How to deliver in an effective way the promise of our human rights and human dignity for all persons, and how specifically to defend the innocent public from invasions of their rights? Many persons have written on the topic of deterrence, and I will not attempt to expand on their thoughts or on the implications of empirical research on deterrence. Deterrence is the *only* moral predicate of *any* criminal sanction. If the threat of execution does not deter, then execution cannot be justified. If the threat of a prison term does not deter, then execution cannot be justified. If fines do not deter, they cannot be justified. Except in the most extreme circumstances, only sanctions that deter can be justified under the law. If bank robbers are immune to deterrents, no sanction of any kind can be justified. If murderers are immune to deterrents, no punishment of any kind can be justified against them. They must be set free. To repeat: deterrence is the only moral predicate of any kind of criminal sanction.

Before leaving the topic of human rights, however, I wish to make a second point, which is that the human rights of the accused and the human rights of the person convicted of crime are every bit as valuable, and every bit as inalienable to use Jefferson's term, as are the rights of the victims or the rights of innocent citizens in general. The purpose of imposing punishment on the guilty criminal is to discourage other persons who might be tempted to abuse the rights of their fellow citizens.

Criminal punishments serve a second function, which is to reassure the public at large that the government and the law are careful of their interests and are dedicated to promoting the general welfare. We punish in order to vindicate the law and the legal process itself, and it is necessary to do that. If the public were to lose faith in their legal institutions and were to question whether police and courts take seriously their duty to maintain order and to defend their rights and their human dignity, all order and all civility would collapse. It would be the law of the jungle, and the institutions that have been created to support human rights would become ineffective. This motive for criminal punishments is usually advanced in the context of a society where crime and mayhem have become so common and widespread that desperate measures are justified to restore some confidence in the law itself, but it is a more general rule.

Widespread breakdown of civil peace is an extremely unusual situation. In general the sort of summary measures that are undertaken—e.g., shooting looters on sight—are so costly, and if they are maintained for long become so counterproductive, that this rationale is of more theoretical than practical interest. I will have occasion to invoke it later on, however, because it is right and it is justice, even if it applies only under special circumstances. Even though it is not the main pillar on which our theory of punishment rests, it is at all times a legitimate proposition. At almost all times, however, and under almost all circumstances, the society is not in fact fighting for its survival and the raw need to reestablish public order is accordingly not sufficient to guide decisions on punishments. I return then to the dogmatic proposition advanced above: the only practical justification for any punishment is deterrence. We punish offenders in order to use them as an example to the wayward of what could happen to them.

There is a third theory of punishment that is followed in some legal traditions, but not in our tradition. That is the proposition that the purpose of punishment is to elicit remorse and penitence. This rationale cannot be reconciled with our doctrine of human rights. Whether the accused feels remorseful or whether he repents and accepts penitence are matters simply outside the law. It is, to put it bluntly, none of our business how the accused feels, either before or after the verdict is rendered. Actually, our legal process does place a great deal of weight on remorse, and indications of remorse have a very large bearing on what punishment will be imposed, because in sentencing, the court seeks to anticipate the prospects for reform and change. Where the prospect is good, they are more inclined to return to felon to society quickly. The threat of drastic punishments may induce the accused to feel remorse, or at least to feign it. Under our law, however, the person can not be forced to repent. He has the right not to feel remorseful.

The alternative—a criminal code which is intended to produce repentance—is based on a moral concept of crime. That is very understandable, in the sense that it seems only natural to build a legal framework on a foundation of morality. Even in our legal system most crimes are also sins—that is to say, they are moral crimes as well as civil crimes—but the law does not exist to enforce the moral law as such.[1] Our law exists to play its part in managing the affairs of the community or the nation in the best interests of the citizens and, especially, to confirm their grant of human rights and human dignity. The morality of the law is the faithfulness with which it preserves and strengthens human rights and dignity. It has no other—no further—moral obligation. A simple, everyday example may help to bring this statement into focus. Gluttony is not merely a sin, it is one of the seven deadly sins. Neither gluttony nor obesity is however a crime. They are mistakes for which the guilty need not answer in this world.

Capital Punishment in the Context of Today's World

In this short essay I wish to reconsider where capital punishment fits in, or should fit in, to our legal system. My orientation is therefore highly theoretical and normative. The matter of capital punishment is, however, inextricably bound up in actual events that occur daily. It is understandably difficult to separate the principles of the law from the myriad practical issues that arise in a particular time and place as the context of those principles. For that reason it makes sense to consider some of that context first.

In America today, and in the Western world in general, capital crimes are relatively rare. By no stretch could we imagine that the law and public order are under attack, or that persons need to go forth daily in the fear of violent death. The number of murders and the number of kidnappings are small enough that well adjusted people do not live in fear. The incidence of rape, as that is defined today, may be high but the incidence of violent rape—what in times past would have been called "rape," to distinguish it from seduction—is apparently tolerable. These are not my personal judgments; they are the public judgement. There is no evidence of the sort of widespread public outrage that would be inevitable if a great many persons were living in daily dread. It is to say the least ironical that the television is positively filled with dramas about violent crime in a way that would be expected to instill fear in the viewing public, and still there is little worrisome evidence of fear.

About a decade ago the nation was gripped by the disgusting spectacle of the O.J. Simpson trial. Nearly everyone would agree that a combination of his money and celebrity status simply bought him acquittal. Yet the public accepts even such a blatant farce to be played out in court. The reason is not hard to find, and it is that murder is not deemed to be a great enough societal problem to demand a more determined response. We can afford, so it seems, to free a lot of the guilty because there just aren't enough of them to be a problem. This is a very persuasive argument, and it has a very significant corollary. I would be hard pressed to counter the proposition that if we cannot even convict O.J., how can we execute anyone else? If the public is not sufficiently outraged by his acquittal, how can it then demand the head of some other, anonymous rapist?

In a society where respect for the law and respect for the rights of other persons prevail, there is a little justification for resorting to execution of criminals. This is what for the most part we have today. What we have in the West is the opposite of a society on the brink, where the most extreme exertions are justified in order to redeem the credibility of the law and of legal process. Our institutions have almost unprecedented credibility and legitimacy. It is not surprising, nor is it at all unjustified, to seek to end executions entirely. I do not advocate that course but it is one of those grey issues that men and women of good will can certainly disagree about. The Pope has weighed in on the side of abolition for precisely the reason I have just summarized, and without doubt it is a very arguable position.[2] At the very least, nearly everyone can agree that there should be very few executions.

There are two cases, however, in which execution is justified even today. The first, and easiest to explain, are cases of horrific crimes that beggar the imagination. John Wayne Gacy—generally thought to have murdered about

35 young men whom he had lured to his home; Jeffrey Dahmer—who over the course of thirteen years killed and ate a large number of his neighbors; Richard Franklin Speck—who murdered six young nurses in their little apartment; and the D.C. snipers—now standing trial for their killing spree. There are other examples also, though they are few. These cases call into question the commitment of the courts and the law to guard the rights of society. They are a direct and conscious affront to our humanity. No response is possible except execution. No other penalty could be justified. Any temporizing raises the question of whether the law actually cares about the citizens at all. What do we say? "Thirty-five dead? Oops!" A law that can not execute a Gacy or a John Muhammed is not law, it is not just, it simply does not care but only takes the path of least resistance.

There is another case that must be addressed. There is no single, homogeneous class of events called "violent crime." There is a wide range of different violent crimes, which demand different treatment under the law. One difference is the number or circumstances of the victims: to murder thirty-five is qualitatively different from killing one person in a brawl. Many of these differences bear on the societal significance of the crime, and society must respond to those differences. There have been many stories lately about abduction and murder of little girls. This crime is highly charged emotionally, and stories evoke perhaps too much emotion and too little thought, but if these cases are at all common they are simply intolerable. We do not need or want to execute a man who shot a bank guard in a holdup in order to deter deviants from abducting and killing little girls. If abduction is common, then we do want to execute some of the more egregious abductors.

The societal threat of a crime depends upon the circumstances that attend it. Indeed it is fair to say that the definition of the crime incorporates those circumstances. Conversely, we cannot be excusing child abductors simply because there have not been many bank robberies lately. It is for jurors, applying the law to particular facts of the case at hand, to make these decisions. The relevant facts, moreover, are those that define how the crime was committed and those that place it in the context of what the community as a whole is facing at that time. This is not to absolve jurors of responsibility for their verdicts. Some are just—most of them—and some are unjust. We have however rightly placed the verdict in their hands.

Some readers, who cling perhaps to a moralistic interpretation of the laws themselves, will object that murder is murder—leaving self-defense aside—and that we as moral judges cannot execute one murderer because his crime frightens us while we suspend that punishment in cases that do not particularly frighten us. This thinking, however, is wrong. The law is not judging moral guilt. The law is managing the affairs of the community and the nation. Some threats demand the most drastic response but others do not. If we do not accept that distinction, we should sentence speeders to prison for life. They are, after all, "guilty."

There is moral guilt just as there is guilt before the law: there is sin as well as crime. But we are not ordained to judge sins. We are not capable of that. We are capable of using our laws and our police and prisons to defend human rights and human dignity, and that is what they are for. This completes the rather lengthy preamble to a presentation of the essential proposals of this essay. We want to turn now to a reconsideration of harsh penalties

in general, in order to ask where capital punishment fits
into that structure.

Other Deterrents

Penal sanctions are levied in stages, from arrest and
arraignment to trial, conviction, and punishment. The research that documents the proposition that the threat of
execution and the threat of long prison terms deter criminal behavior makes another point that is of importance
here. The harshness of punishments would be irrelevant
in itself if a significant percentage of criminals either
were never arrested or, if arrested, were set free by the
courts. In quantitative terms, the threat of arrest and the
threat of conviction are actually to be the most effective
deterrents. This has several important implications.

The most immediate one is that the punishments
meted out to criminals are already very harsh. The
greater effect is achieved not by increasing them, but by
implementing them. If the severity of punishments had
the effect of deterring juries from convicting guilty defendants, the legal system could actually increase deterrence
by lightening the sentences and thus raising the odds of
conviction. The devil is in the numbers, of course. It matters by how much the sentences are reduced and by how
much the risk of conviction rises, but if the probability of
conviction was to rise, in percentage terms, by anywhere
nearly as much as sentences were shortened in percentage terms, the overall effect would be a deterrent to
crime. This is an interesting proposition, and one that the
Pope has taken into account. I will argue, on quite other
grounds, that actually prison terms are too long. If in ad-

70

dition this scenario is the reality, then of course the point would be strengthened.

There is, on grounds of human rights, a limit to the applicability of this idea. There is a limit to what any society is and should be willing to do in the form of police work and the regulation of daily life in order to achieve deterrence. The criminal law is not some pure abstraction because the action of the law may itself jeopardize the rights of the citizenry.

It would in principle be possible to watch every citizen every minute of the day, and whenever he violated some law or other to give him a sharp electric shock, as well as providing valuable video tape to assist the prosecution. That is to say, it is possible to treat every person as a criminal, but it is the grossest violation of his human rights—among which is counted the right to liberty—and of his human dignity. It is a greater wrong to punish the innocent by taking away their human rights than it is to punish the guilty. Indeed, we find little dissent to the rule that we will not sacrifice the innocent in order to preserve the guilty. Not only is deterrence the only moral justification for any punishment, it constitutes deterrence as the only moral civil response to crime. I have already expanded on this thesis in the previous chapter.

In a free society, which is to say a society in which the rights of the public are preserved and practiced, it is inevitable that many crimes will go unnoticed, and of those that are detected many will not lead to an arrest or a conviction. That is in effect the price we pay for our rights and dignity. It is therefore equally inevitable that the punishments imposed on those convicted of crime will be harsh, and that at the margin it will seem that greater effect could be achieved by raising the odds of conviction of offenders than by stiffening the penalties.

The conclusion is that in modern society it is possible to improve the effectiveness of the police and courts in ways that do not violate the rights of the citizens, and that of course where possibilities of this kind exist they should be used. Nevertheless, there are very strict limits to what is justifiable when the rights of the general public are threatened.

Prison: Time and Hard Time

Since the preamble has been long, let me get immediately to the one really essential idea. Opponents of capital punishment frequently predicate their position in moralistic terms: they assert that society and the law do not have the "right" to take a human life. I do not find that simplistic proposition to be at all moral. It is simply jargon that can cover a multitude of beliefs that range from the truly moral to the most self-serving. However, it also lays down a challenge for everyone to think about what the law has the right to take.

The only punishment that I cannot justify morally is life in prison without hope of parole. Wholly apart from any other consideration, it *is* capital punishment; it is taking the convict's life, but it takes it in a hypocritical way, one day at a time. Life imprisonment without realistic hope of parole can never be justified for any crime. Society and the law do not have the right to imprison anyone for his or her whole life. That is the only unacceptable punishment. I need not speak about death by torture, which is also unjustifiable, but that is never practiced in the West. If we accept this premise—and it is hard to avoid the inference that life in prison is taking the life—then we are forced to rethink *everything* about how we punish serious crime. As we think this through, we will be led to recognize other circumstances—other than the ones mentioned in the previous section—in which execution is the right punishment. The fact remains however that when a nation is at peace and where the laws have great legitimacy and credibility, executions will be rare.

If life without realistic hope of parole is unjustifiable, then it would in principle be sufficient to establish by law that regardless of the crime involved, everyone has a right to regular parole hearings starting no later than some fixed number of years. For instance, the law could stipulate that every convict has the right to petition for parole every year, after twenty years in penitentiary. This would not substitute for other parole provisions. Someone, for instance, sentenced to five years for aggravated assault would still be able to petition for parole after a couple of years or even fewer. It would simply fix an absolute maximum of time that anyone could be imprisoned without a parole hearing.

In principle I could simply stop here, and propose this modest tinkering with the penal code, but that actually misses the point. In fact it misses several points. On the one side, many persons would protest that for this case or for that one, twenty years is simply not enough. They would protest that this person would or could never be released. We cannot—or at least we are not supposed to—console them with the thought that in fact the poor soul will never actually be paroled. That is only sidestepping the issue. The guarantee is for a *realistic* hope of parole, and not just for a charade of a hearing. If we are true, then, to the principle that we must be willing to release everyone after twenty years—the exact number is of course only illustrative, though it really cannot be larger than about twenty years—we are forced to think seriously about what the prison term is supposed to accomplish.

It has two functions. First, it is a deterrent. If it is not a deterrent, we should stop sending persons to penitentiary at all. Systematic empirical research documents, however, that long prison terms are a deterrent.[3] We are not willing to release all criminals from prison after a year or even two. For serious crimes, that is not a sufficient deterrent. Something like twenty years, however, is effectively an eternity. No one who commits a crime has the slightest idea what he will be like twenty years in the future, or what losing the next twenty years of his life will mean. It is as good as his whole life. It may be that some criminals are so delusional that they think twenty years in the pen is okay, but that thirty or forty is intolerable: in other words there may be some person for whom only that third or fourth decade is a sufficient deterrent. But people like this have to be so few in number that, bearing in mind that we will never deter everyone, we should simply ignore them. Any rational person, if he can be deterred at all, would be deterred by twenty years.

Secondly, the prison term is a time to reform. The law does not particularly care whether the convict repents. That is an important matter for him and much depends on it, but it is not important for the law. We do however want the person to lose interest in serious crime, and ideally to acquire usable skills that can support him in society: not only job skills but personal skills as well. If in reality he is going to do that, he has to have the hope of getting out of penitentiary early enough actually to build a life in society. For that reason, I would propose that twenty years is actually too long.

In a previous chapter, I recommended a limit of

74

twelve years, which may be shorter than most citizens would accept. Realistically, some term in the middle would be satisfactory. The so-called "Three strikes and you're out" law comes close to what I propose. A person convicted of a major felony even for the second time can reasonably expect to get parole in a relatively few years, certainly far fewer than twenty years. If it is wrong to take a person's whole life by taking it one day at a time, then it is also wrong—though less serious—to take most of his life or a lot of his life. A tradeoff must be found because the sentence must deter, but effective terms between five and ten years are plausible.

This disposition of matters is consistent with both the needs of the penal system and with the human rights of the guilty. I do not think, however, that it is the best penal system. I would propose a slightly different one. This proposal expands on a proposal that I first made in the essay "Justice and Deterrence," where I suggested twelve years as the maximum. I have argued above that the state does not have the right to assign a convict to penitentiary for the rest of his life without a reasonable prospect of parole. Actually, I would advance a stronger statement. There should be some maximum term—fifteen years, for instance—which is the maximum time for which the state can keep any person in penitentiary. If the penitentiary is supposed to reform, there must be some term which is deemed enough for this purpose.

The radical aspect of this idea is that the maximum—the fifteen years, to use my example—is not the maximum sentence for a given crime. It is the maximum number of years that anyone can be held in penitentiary, over the course of his life. The precise number of years is not something for me or anyone else to dictate. It must be settled on by the community at large. I will continue to use fifteen years because that is the term that I would vote for, but the penal code is not a personal decision. It is a community decision. We collectively will decide, but while the public at large is left to fix the maximum stay in penitentiary, there must be some allowable upper limit on this choice. Perhaps twenty-five years could be accepted as an absolute maximum, subject to the will of the community to fix the maximum at a lower number of years. The maximum must be set so as to allow the person who is released the time to build a life and to make some contribution to society. That is what reform is for.

Most felonies carry a sentence of fewer than ten years, and even before that time has elapsed, the convict may petition for parole. There is no need to change any of those sentencing guidelines. The maximum applies to actual time served. Thus, for instance, if someone convicted of armed robbery and sentenced to twelve years is actually released on parole after three years, he has spent three of his allotted fifteen years in penitentiary.

Some prisoners will not reform after fifteen years. That is actually quite remarkable, because fifteen years is a terribly long time in penitentiary. The man who emerges is in many ways an entirely different man from the one who entered. That is even truer because he will very likely have amassed his fifteen years behind bars as the result of several convictions. Only the most serious offenses carry a term of fifteen years or more, and even then he may have been released early on parole. It is not easy to actually spend fifteen years in a penitentiary. After fifteen years in prison, over the span of perhaps twenty years or more, there is simply nothing more that the penal system can do with him or for him. If he has not reformed his life in that time, under the harsh conditions of the penitentiary, it is extremely unlikely that he will reform in more years. On the other hand, if he has reformed his life, then there is no reason to hold him, and there is every reason to return him to a society that he now wants to belong to. He would be released by law at that time.

It is very possible that after so many years in prison, he will not be able to support himself and to make his way in society. He might even resort to petty crime to get by, even though he has turned his back on the sort of grave felonies that put him in prison for so many years. Persons of this type can be dealt with in either of two ways. One is that they can be pensioned off: given a modest stipend to keep them going and regular interaction with social case-workers to make sure that he is at least harmless. The other approach—perhaps a complementary one—is to assign hopeless cases to some sort of minimum security penitentiary for the remainder of their lives. While confined to the grounds, they would lead lives as complete and normal as possible, with jobs, perhaps even families, and all the wholesome components of a normal life.

There is another possibility however, which is that the convict returns to a life of violent crime even after he has served the maximum time. By violent crime I mean here all those crimes which put human life in jeopardy. Not only murder and aggravated battery, but rape, abduction, armed robbery or any felony committed with a deadly weapon, and similar offenses. It is not material whether in that particular case anyone died. What matters is that life was put in jeopardy, because the difference between threat and act is luck; by intent they are the same crime. These criminals I would execute.

I would execute them for threatening or for actually causing the death of innocents. I would execute them as a deterrent to violent criminals, to see that either they will reform or they will die. I would execute them in order to preserve the penal code as I have presented it, including its promise of mercy and a new start in life for those who do reform. If we would fail to execute hardened criminals, the whole system would surely unravel. The demand for longer sentences for all criminals and for life sentences for many of them would be impossible to resist. We would end again with prisons filled with hopeless men, caged and put away for the rest of their lives.

This is a very simple idea, and as I indicated above not altogether different from the Three Strikes penal system that we have today. But it would result in somewhat more executions, but in far fewer lives wasted and lost in cages, and in a more effective deterrent as well.

Related Matters: Appeals and the Popular Media

There are two issues that are related to the penal system and its actual workings that I will speak to here. One of them is appeals to higher courts, and the other is the way crime is treated in the media.

Appeals

No aspect of the law does more to bring it into contempt than the endless appeals brought by any defendant who can afford high-priced counsel. One message that they send is very clearly one of justice for sale at a price. Another is that in the scramble for cash, the lawyers are winning and the law is losing. The purpose of the law—of legal process and legal sanctions against the guilty—is to vindicate the law in the eyes of the citizens that it was created to serve. Endless appeals convey the opposite message: that the lawyers have hijacked the process and the courts for their own ends and in disregard of the needs and the rights of the citizens.

In response I suggest something like the following. It is, to say the least, a mystery how there could possibly be more appeals than trials. After the trial, there is a chain of appeals that might rise even to the Supreme Court. Granted. Then how can there be other appeals? What is left to appeal? Wouldn't there have to be another trial to form the basis for a new appeal? Some appeals result in a remand of the matter and a retrial, so it will sometimes happen that the whole sequence from trial to appeal will be repeated, but in reality this is very rare. In any case, it is perfectly comprehensible. What is not comprehensible is a legal process in which one can appeal rulings made at trials that have never even happened.

The Media

The media—particularly the television and films—are fascinated with crime and punishment. The impression one would get is that of a country and a society in the throes of a virulent crime wave. Many of the newest shows feature military courts, leading to the impression that even the armed services are not exempt from the crime wave. This is certainly not accurate. There is no such crime wave. But the constant drumbeat of crime and punishment, of threat and defense, surely distorts public perceptions of incidence of the problem of grave crime.

Exactly which steps the community takes to manage criminally depends, and should depend, on how threatened the public is. If crime is viewed as not a big problem, mild punishments are appropriate. If the threat of victimization is high, stern measures are called for. We don't punish criminals because in some abstract sense they are guilty, or because in a moralistic sense they are guilty. We punish them because we are threatened by them.

In an ideal world, the perception of threat and the reality of threat would be the same, but in this world they do not have to be the same. It seems to me that the incessant reenacting of scenes of victimization on the television leads to fear and to unreasonably strict penalties. This is especially so since each episode culminates in the reenacting of a trial or some other legal process in which the guilty are brought to the dock and justice ultimately prevails. The message is then not only that the barbarians are at the proverbial gates, to borrow a phrase, but that our courts and our law have the answer for the deep fear that this thought provokes. I can think of few services one could render to the American public that would be more valuable than to put in perspective the actual risks from various crimes, and also some sense of the actual effectiveness of the courts and legal process. If we had a clearer idea of how big a problem crime is and of how reliably the law addresses it, we could as a community put into place a penal system that really serves the end of defending the rights of offenders, victims, and the whole community.

Notes

1. This proposition seems on its face to be a rejection of morality, but it is not. It is rather simply a recognition of the limitations of law, courts, and government. It was expressed without apology by, amongst others, St. Thomas More—the esteemed "Man for All Seasons."

2. This single comment does not begin to do justice to the Pope's position, but it is the one element of it that bears on my topic. His starting point is that because we are in a time of domestic peace and tranquility we have a chance to show mercy and temperance toward criminals, in an effort to give them time and a chance to reform their lives. See his encyclical letter "Evangelium Vitae," promulgated 25 March, 1995. I agree wholeheartedly with this, even though I do not support abolition. The practical fact, in my opinion, is that it is not the one execution that is hard to justify, but the ten who are locked away in prison cells for most of what remains of their lives.
3. *Viz.* Isaac Ehrlich and Gary Becker, cited above.

4

Crime, Punishment, and Reform

In many legal systems, inducing contrition on the part of the criminal is considered a legitimate goal of the criminal law. In the three preceding essays, "Justice and Deterrence," "Deterrence and Prevention," and "Another Way," I have argued that achieving contrition is not a proper goal. In plainer terms, it is not a goal of the legal system to make the guilty confess or express remorse or shame or promise to reform. There remains however much more that ought to be said on this topic, and particularly about what is the place of reform[1] in the penal system.

Why is it not the job of the legal process to induce sorrow and contrition for crimes?

The reason is quite simple. It is not the job of the courts to improve the citizens, to make them better human beings. The job of the law and the courts is to induce them—"make them" is too strong a term because of course there will always be violations—not to hurt their fellow citizens. Measures that promote that end are in principle valid, but measures that serve other ends are not valid at all. The law and the courts are not moral authorities and they are not gods, and thus it is not their task to mend the conscience of the accused.

In writing this, I am not dismissing the need for and the value of remorse and contrition. The demands of the conscience, and the need to have a conscience, are far more important for the individual person than are all the laws in all the books of law in the whole world. It is conscience that separates us from the animals. Until however we have a legal education that confers the ability to read minds, laws and courts and legal processes are simply not capable to judge such matters. The law deals with visible facts and evidence. Its goal is to encourage behavior conducive to the common good, and it has nothing to say about what causes the citizens to behave that way.

As I noted in a previous essay, it used to be advanced as a justification for the death penalty that the threat of impending death extended to the criminal one final opportunity to repent. For those so lacking in conscience that they would commit heinous crimes, perhaps seeing the day of their own death upon them might—if nothing else—would reawaken their conscience and force them to acknowledge their guilt before it would be too late. This is not by any means a cruel or reckless motive for severe punishment. It should not be confused, in particular, with vengeance. On the contrary, repentance is good for everyone, and repentance of the gravest crimes is the most desirable of all. It does not benefit anyone else in any way, but it restores the humanity of the penitent and restores his human conscience. Vengeance, by contrast, causes bystanders to participate in the crime and to extend and perpetuate it, while it merely makes the accused another victim. Thus if contrition is a result of any punishment, of any degree of seriousness, that is a good in and through itself [a cause of other goods]. However, it remains true that it is not a proper consideration in a court of law. Even if it is a desirable outcome for the guilty criminal, it is not an adequate reason to punish and it is not a proper factor in choosing a form of punishment.

Design for Reform

Even those who endorse the preceding statements are very inclined to associate personal reform and remorse with the criminal process and with criminal sanctions. We cannot construct a legal regime without taking reform into account. The citizens are well aware of the importance of remorse. Juries are usually reported to have been influenced by the expression of remorse on the part of the accused, or by the absence of such an expression. It is entirely reasonable to ask what it is that the jurors are looking for, and why.

It seems obvious that one thing they are looking at is the power of the example that the convict gives. The goal of the criminal law is above all to prevent—by any effective means, although deterrence is the bedrock—more, similar events in the future. One implication of expressions of remorse is that through them the convicted person publicly rejects and denounces his own crimes. Other persons who might be tempted to emulate him are therefore denied the confirmation of his example. One reason that organized resistance—so-called "terrorism"—is so hard to combat is that it is cloaked in a mantle of extralegal justification. Captured activists are viewed as soldiers and when punished they become martyrs. This constitutes, as nearly as one could devise, a design for perpetuating the resistance and for preventing reform.[2] How effective an admission of guilt is, how much it removes the glamor of crime, and how many future offenses are reduced as a result, is a practical matter, the public is inclined to attach a considerable value to expressions of contrition.

There is another side of public contrition, which raises significant issues regarding law and punishment. It seems that a person who violates any law is thought to have in some degree forfeited his right to the sympathy of the public. The implied judgement seems to be: "Fine him; jail him; hang him. We no longer have any care about him. We wash our hands of him." In reality, of course, the judgement comes in degrees. No one wants to hang anyone for spitting on the sidewalk, but the thought is fundamentally the same. An expression of remorse and contrition acts in effect to reconnect the convict with the community. We begin again to take his interests into consideration. Whatever hurts him hurts us too to some degree. This is a natural, but also a dangerous tendency, and should not really be encouraged. It sets the community, the society, as a moral judge, and it does so on very shaky practical grounds. It is not very hard to feign remorse. Even if it were, however, the public has no right to make such judgements. The convict is equally a member of the community and equally entitled to respect and human dignity. It is because of the separation of church and state that we acknowledge that the state and the community are not moral judges. The community does not know who is good and who is bad; it does not know who is righteous and who is wicked. It is not legitimate then for the public to bend the law and its enforcement to perceptions of moral worth.

There is a third aspect of expressions of remorse that should carry and does carry the most weight. When he expresses contrition for his crimes, the guilty one is asserting a desire for reform: a rejection of his former way of life and a desire to live differently in the future. Leniency toward the contrite is a reward for those who appear likely to reform themselves, and it is therefore an incentive to reform. This seems paradoxical. On the one hand, the courts and the law have no commission to promote feelings of remorse, and yet they do routinely reward the contrite. These principles are not however incompatible and there is no paradox as long as we keep in mind the difference between remorse and reform.

Reform Is Central to the Administration of Justice

The justification, and if you will the morality, of criminal sanctions is deterrence, because it is intended to discourage future similar incidents. The value of reform is not to be found in the *fact* of sanctions. It is rather a determinant of the *form* that they take.

Criminal sanctions are of three fundamentally different types: fines, imprisonment, and death. These approaches correlate with the needs and the prospects for reform. Fines are appropriate in cases where the offender, and other prospective offenders, need a simple disincentive to engage in a particular illegal activity. Ordinary traffic violations for instance are controlled by direct enforcement—police patrols—and fines. This is because the offender, while needing a jolt of disincentive, does not need a "reform" in the true sense. We are not trying, in the case of traffic offenses, to effect a significant change in his whole outlook on life. That is not needed, but a moderate swat for running a red light or whatever is called for. So, fines are used when there is no case for trying to change the offender and thus no pressing need for reform.

Imprisonment is called for precisely when significant reform is needed: when a significant change in the offender's life and attitudes is needed. The prison is the place where reform is supposed to be accomplished. I say "supposed to be," of course, because there is no guarantee that it will be effective. It is the place where we try to bring about reform.

It is well known that no one reforms until he has acknowledged the need to reform. Reform is not a coat of whitewash that we can apply as we wish. It has to be a deep-seated change in the person himself. It is usually, therefore, accompanied by remorse, but that is not necessary. A convicted thief who is confined to the penitentiary might be inclined to take advantage of the educational facilities there so that when he is released he can earn an honest living. It is not required that he renounce theft as an occupation, as a matter of principle. All that is necessary is that he lay aside theft, as being an inferior way for him to make a living. Reform is not the same thing as remorse and contrition; either one can occur without the other. The prison is only a place for effecting reform. However, to repeat a remark above, remorse undoubtedly promotes reform.

Execution is provided in cases of grave crimes—crimes that take life or that endanger the community in ways that can lead to other heinous crimes—and in which the need for deterrence overrides the goal of reform. This is of course the reason that someone convicted of a heinous crime may express remorse and contrition. He is asserting a willingness to reform. Persons who reject reform inevitably place themselves in a position where the goal of reform is deemed to be pointless for them. They risk being judged to be persons whose only remaining prospect is to promote deterrence. Mere defiance on the part of the convict is not a sufficient justification for execution, because the law and the society have to be the last judges of that, and be guided by consideration of the needs of the community apart from the desires of the convicted person. Even if a man, convicted of driving 55 mph in a 25 mph zone, proclaims that he will not change, he could not be executed except under the most extraordinary circumstances.[3]

At the same time, there are circumstances in which even a contrite criminal would be executed. It is a matter of the degree of urgency in achieving deterrence. Actually, this is a more common situation than it seems. Most criminals who are executed for their crimes are led in the end to accept the justice of the sentence and to feel remorse. It is a very rare convict who goes to his death defiant. It is not, however, the goal or purpose of the law and the courts to promote contrition. They exist to manage the affairs of the society, and in this instance to exact the penalty of death in those cases when the need for deterrence outweighs the goal of reform.

All criminal penalties are justified, as a matter of law, by their capacity to deter other people. Of the three forms of punishment—fines, prison, or death—it is not always the case that fines are the least severe and death the most. A fine that impoverishes a person and his family for life is a far more onerous sanction than a month or even a year in prison. Fines therefore can be among the most powerful and efficient deterrents. What distinguishes these forms most surely is how they stand in regard to the goal of effecting reform of the convict. The penitentiary is the place of reform and consignment to it is intended to achieve the reform of the convict.

If Prison Exists for Reform, What Then Follows?

If, or rather **since,** the penitentiary exists to reform, the nature of prison sentences must be consistent with that goal. This does not mean that they have to be assured to achieve that objective. Many felons simply are not going to be reformed, but we do not fashion the prisons, however, on the basis of the quirks of individual convicts. We design them to promote the objectives of the law and of the society. Two issues are paramount in this regard. First, how do we reconcile reform and deterrence in penitentiary, and second, how do we achieve—or attempt to achieve—deterrence when reform is not a consideration?

Take the second question first, because it is an easier matter. I mentioned before that for grave or heinous crimes, the deterrent of execution may override the desire to promote reform. It is much more often the case that the offense is not nearly grave enough to invoke the death penalty, and that we want simply deterrence without reform. The example of traffic offenses is of this type. It would be misleading to leave that as the final word, however, because it suggests that this is the situation of minor infractions. That is far from the case. The courts also levy fines in cases like business fraud and other so-called "white collar" crimes. The principle at work is that if the fine can be raised high enough to accomplish deterrence that is the best avenue. The culprits—often men and women of wealth and education—are simply not good prospects for reform. There is almost nothing that they can learn in the penitentiary that would make them less likely to defraud anyone in the future. We simply don't know how to reform them. It might be that the deterrent value of a spell in the penitentiary is needed as a supplement to fines. In these cases prison serves only the deterrent capacity, when there is no intention—as in these cases there should be no intention—to impose death. Some felons are sent to prison even though no reform is expected. By the same token, however, we always prefer to use fines in these cases to achieve the necessary degree of deterrence.

The first question is really a couple of different questions. One of them is, in effect, whether reform replaces deterrence. I have already observed that it does not in white collar crimes. Within the prison walls, moreover, deterrence has a place. The convicts are in most cases not easy persons to deal with, and so the officers are given many instruments to force the inmates to comply with the commands and goals of the warden. Prison is not university. Many crimes, in particular, are committed in prison, including murder. They must be dealt with as crimes. The purpose of the prison, however, is to induce the inmates to adopt the goals of the authorities.

It is obvious that no convict is going to reform unless he is given the realistic hope of putting that reform to work. It is necessary that within the prison he is treated as a human being with all the rights and even freedoms feasible. It is even more necessary that he have a realistic prospect of walking away from the penitentiary a free man, able to enjoy the freedom and the benefits that reform provides. Otherwise, he simply has no incentive to adopt the goal of reform. Things like solitary confinement and, more importantly, unlimited sentences defeat the whole purpose of prison.

Let me repeat this important point: the very idea of unlimited sentences contradicts what prison is intended to accomplish. Even terribly long sentences defeat the purpose of prison. It is not enough simply to assure a convict that he will eventually walk free. He must walk free with enough of his life remaining to make the promise of reform a real value to him. It was on this account that I proposed in an earlier chapter that the law fix a certain absolute limit to the number of years for which anyone could be sent to prison during his life. The length of that term should, moreover, be at least loosely tied to some idea of how long it might take to reform a very difficult case. I proposed—more in the spirit of starting the discussion than to settle it—that fifteen years should be long enough. Whatever the number, it is the maximum numbers of years of a person's life that he or she could be confined to prison.

Judgmental Release: Parole

The penal code provides for release of prisoners before their maximum term has been completed. In outline, the law provides for extremely long sentences, but with a right to petition for early release on parole.

This is not always available. In recent years sentences that cannot be reduced—"life without parole" and "life on death row"—have cropped up in the code. As I have argued elsewhere in this set of essays, unlimited sentences cannot be justified either legally or morally. It is a subterfuge: simply taking life one day at a time. Life on death row is particularly outrageous, because it amounts to a life in solitary confinement. The convict is let out of his cell for only a short interval—perhaps an hour—each day. The rest of his time, he is suspended in solitary confinement. This is not merely taking life one day at a time, it is tantamount to torturing the man to death.

Most sentences are for a limited term and parole is available. Nonetheless, the exceptionally large prison population in America today implies that, on average, stays in prison are excessive. This may be due in part to the poor job we do in promoting reform and in making the resources needed for rehabilitation available. Whatever the reason, it is evidence that the penal system is failing to accomplish its goal of reform. We don't want reformed criminals to be sitting around penitentiaries; we want them out in society making a living and a life. There is no way to avoid asking whether the promise of parole is achieving its purpose.

I do not claim to be able to answer this question, or even to illuminate it, beyond these few remarks. The scholars and courts and policy makers of our penal system wrestle with these issues every day. There is no reason in principle that the right of parole and the actual implementation of parole review should not be bringing about the results intended, and one can easily make a case for continued tinkering rather than a drastic overhaul. Nonetheless, if we are failing to inspire convicts to choose reform and to discipline themselves to the hard work that it requires, we need to do something different. I have proposed something rather drastically different, which is that instead of parole, prison sentences be fixed, and fixed at shorter terms than are the maximums today. This delivers a credible message to every convict that he will have an opportunity to enjoy a real life before too much of his life has passed. This is, as it were, the carrot.

The stick is that if he continues a life of crime and demonstrates that he has rejected the goal of reform, his life may be forfeit. There are many crimes that are tantamount to murder: dealing hard drugs, armed robbery, and forcible rape are all examples. Drugs kill the victim as surely as bullets do. The only difference between armed robbery and robbery/murder is luck. The same is true of rape and murder/rape. We do not have to absolve violent criminals because they get lucky.

It is entirely too easy for society to lock the convicted criminals away and forget them in warehouses for the rejected. Problem solved: get tough on crime. This cannot be justified on the grounds of human rights. The criminals are also citizens and beneficiaries of the same inalienable human rights that Thomas Jefferson listed in the Declaration of Independence. The many men and women who deal on a daily basis with the courts and the penal system and who have dedicated their lives to the rights of the criminals and the rights of the society are in the best position to assess how best to manage the penal system to promote reform. I defer without question to their combined experience and good will. I think, however, that it is safe to say that they would on the whole agree that convicts spend too much time in prison.

There is one aspect of the parole review that is clearly out of place, and that sometimes contributes in effect to revoking the right to parole. That is the practice of taking testimony in the parole review from interested parties: victims or survivors of victims and other persons with a comparable ax to grind. That only diverts the hearing from its proper focus, which is on whether the convict has made sufficient progress in reforming his life to merit release. Allowing interested parties to influence the outcome violates the principle that criminal prosecutions are matters between the accused and the society as a whole. In this context it has the further flaw that it authorizes the parole panel to extend prison terms despite the best efforts of the convict to adopt the goals of the law and of the institution. The effect can only be to undermine the credibility of the parole promise and to discourage reform.

It is revealing that prison terms meted out in America are much longer than the terms in other advanced countries for the same crimes. Everyone accepts the fact that it is often necessary to "get tough on crime." Getting tough on criminals is a necessary tactic: a means to an end. But getting tough only on reform and rehabilitation is an end in itself.

Notes

1. The term "rehabilitation" is often used as a synonym for what I am calling "reform," and the reader is free to use that term. The two are not, however, exactly synonymous, and it is reform, rather than rehabilitation, that is the goal. The difference between them is that reform refers to a fundamental change that starts from the convict himself. Rehabilitation, by contrast, is something produced from outside, by the penal system.
2. History has provided many examples of what we deem to be valid resistance to an immoral legal code. We accordingly use terms like "reform" and "resistance" with reservations in this contest. All legal systems have however fundamentally, and in outline, the same objectives and the same methods, so the example is still a valuable one for our purposes.
3. We cannot rule out *a priori* a death sentence for speeding. It is conceivable that hazardous driving can be so grave a danger to the community—putting so many lives at risk—that it would be a capital offense. Hopefully, however, this is no more than a theoretical proposition. No one would want to live in such a world.

5

The Choice of Sanctions: The Example of the Scott Peterson Case

The murder of Laci Peterson, who was an expectant mother at the time of her death, agitated the press for a period of months. After nearly six months of taking evidence and testimony, a jury in California convicted her husband, Scott Peterson, of the murder. One of their findings was that the murder took place because she was pregnant; that the husband did not want Laci to bring their child into the world. The jury not only found Scott Peterson guilty, it found that in this case, the crime merits a sentence of death. I think that this case has a lot to teach about the death penalty and under what circumstances it is indicated. While I recognize at the outset that I only know the facts of the case from whatever has been revealed in the press, I find the verdict of the jury to be quite justifiable. There are really two factors that I would draw attention to in this case: the defendant's apparent lack of remorse and the fact that the killing involved an unborn child.

Remorse

The jurors who were interviewed by the press after rendering their verdict all pointed to the defendant's lack of any apparent remorse as being a important factor in their reasoning. That is a matter that they were competent to judge, and that I have no way to second guess. They are right that lack of remorse may change the nature of the crime itself, and may tip the scales of justice toward a sentence of death.

Murder of a Pregnant Woman

It is in any case more significant that Scott Peterson apparently set out with the express purpose of killing both his wife and their child. That is a fact—the jurors found it to be a fact—that fundamentally changes the nature of the crime and makes it more serious than it might otherwise be.

To repeat a proposition that I advanced elsewhere, the legal definition of a crime includes all of the circumstances under which it took place. If, in this case, the wife had not been pregnant it would have been a different crime. In the actual case, there were two victims and in general the number of victims is also an important factor defining the crime. In this case, however, the essential difference with this crime is not the number of victims. The essential fact is that he murdered his wife in order to kill their child.

Most people would suppose that the murder of pregnant women is an extremely rare event, and that their murder by the child's father is extraordinarily rare. The frequency of a given heinous crime is an important consideration in sentencing. We reach for our strongest deterrents to combat crimes that are not only despicable in themselves, but that also represent an attack on society at large. Rare crimes do not easily meet this test, and the death sentence is consequently very hard to justify. In the case at hand therefore we want to know more about the frequency of paternal murder.

This is a topic that has apparently gone unnoticed until very recently, and the data that are needed to address it definitively do not exist. The victimization statistics for murder do not ordinarily identify whether a female victim was pregnant at the time of her death. In the last couple of years, however, some forensic criminologists have taken an interest in this issue and have reconstructed data for the last few years. Their best estimate is that about three hundred pregnant women are the victims of homicide each year, and that the number has been rising.

The scope of this crime is moreover considerably broader than the number of murdered women would imply. These murders occur because the mother wants her child and the father does not and is willing to kill mother and child to be free of them. This leads us naturally to ask how many women terminate pregnancies because they fear that the father may kill them and the child. About a third of elective abortions are performed on young, single women, about a half a million abortions each year. How many of those "choices" were made under duress? It is unquestionably true that some abortions are chosen by the mother out of fear that the father will harm her and her child. We do not know whether this is common or rare, but we do know that whether sentencing decisions should pay attention to it is very much dependent on the frequency. Harsh penalties, those dominated by the need to deter at all costs, are justified by crimes that attack the society as a whole. If fathers rarely abused or killed the mothers of their children, in order to free themselves of the burden of the children, then that crime would not be societal problem and leniency would be appropriate. If however this is a widespread crime, and if it motivates a large number of elective abortions as well, then it is an attack on the society as a whole. It would not be hard to imagine that some hundreds of thousands of children die each year for this reason. Guesswork is never a substitute for knowledge, and so we need to know more of the actual facts, but juries have to render verdicts today. The Peterson jury has decided, and I for one cannot say that they acted rashly.

For rare and peculiar crimes—for what one might call "Agatha Christie murders"—the value that the law and society place on human life urges leniency toward the guilty party. The living—those available to serve on the jury—cannot legitimately assert that they or people like them are threatened by like crimes. For widespread crimes, however, our appreciation of the value of human life demands that deterrence be given the highest priority in sentencing, and it therefore may demand a sentence of death. What is leniency and restraint in exceptional cases may be only self-doubt and cowardice in other circumstances, when the crime is only one of many other crimes of the same type.

Part Two

On the Separation of Church and State

6

Abortion under the Law

The public debate over abortion and the law raises essential matters of the separation of church and state. While both sides allude to the doctrine of separation, not nearly enough discussion has been devoted to this subject. In this essay, I propose to consider it in some detail and, in consequence, ideally to raise or even to settle some important questions that have remained in the shadows for too long.

Separation of Church and State: Autonomy of the State

The separation of church and state is a doctrine first enunciated by the Catholic church, on the basis of clear scriptural passages from both the gospels and the epistles of the early apostles. Notwithstanding the clear commitment to the principle, the turbulent history of Europe and the Mediterranean area, especially during the dark ages, and the relative strength and stability of the institution of the church—not to mention the great wisdom and learning exhibited by so many leaders of the church—drew her into many areas of law that we now, in better times, view as the province of the state. The premise of separation is that the state is instituted for the benefit and defense of the civil society. For that reason, government is inherently limited and the totalitarian aberrations of modern times are fundamentally a violation of the true constitution of the state.

The inherent limitation of the state was recognized by Saint Thomas Aquinas in his famous dictum: "A bad law is null and void, not binding on the citizen." By "bad law" he did not mean an unpopular or inconvenient one. He was speaking rather more specifically about a law that promotes injustice or that violates the limitations that bind the civil authority. This doctrine, first promulgated about eight hundred years ago, roughly contemporaneous with the Magna Carta, is one of the essential insights into the nature of the state and remains as true and binding today as it was then.

Just as the state has its proper tasks, the church does also.[1] One limitation of course is that only a part of the population are members of the church, and relations between the church and the rest of the people are necessarily very limited, by comparison with the active communicants. Within the ambit of the communicants, the church is still fundamentally limited by her very nature, which is to be a service to the people. One form that the service takes is to be a sort of conscience and guide and in that capacity, the church addresses all sorts of moral issues, but the church is not a government and has no police powers.

The cornerstone of separation is, then, that both church and state are defined by their missions to serve the people and the community, and both are inherently limited by their constitutions. Unlimited church is as foreign to us as is unlimited government, although in fact world history is littered with violations of both. It is clear that on either side, the Catholic church and the American government have been comparatively speaking models of good behavior in this regard, though neither has been perfect.

Morality and Law

Church and state share an interest in human behavior, and each has its own proper concept of crime. Civil crime—the province of the government—comprehends actions that are a threat to the civil order and that undermine legitimate human rights. Moral crime, otherwise known as sin, comprehends a much wider category of actions or attitudes that violate the divine gift of our human nature: actions and attitudes that attack our humanity and that attack the humanity of our neighbors. We usually use the term "crime" to refer to civil crime, and the term "sin" to mean moral crime. I will do so. These two concepts, of sin and crime, are as distinct as the separation of church and state. As evidence of the distinction, it is not hard to adduce examples that are crime but not sin, and examples—far more numerous—of sins that are not crimes.

For the most part, civil crime is also sinful but there are exceptions. One such exception is highway speed limits. They are established by government at various levels in order to regulate the flow of traffic. At times they are distorted in order to generate revenues for the locality, without regard to the best interests of the driving public, but for the most part traffic regulations are legitimate and appropriate. They are not, however, moral law. The moral law looks to the purposes and intentions of our actions, while the traffic code looks only to the outcomes.

Speeding is illegal; reckless driving is immoral. To drive fast on an empty road is illegal but not necessarily immoral. Moral judgement depends upon whether the driver is endangering himself or others or their property, and not on the posted speeds as such. The public does have a moral duty of compliance with all legitimate civil authority, but the fact that the authorities are in fact very lax about enforcing the speed limits makes clear that they are not actually understood to be absolutes. Rather, they constitute an attempt to discourage reckless driving and a way to assign guilt, in a *prima facie* way, in case of an accident.

Examples of sins that are not crimes are very abundant. The essential element of a crime is that it is an attack on the society and on the civil rights of other persons. Sin, by contrast, encompasses both actions and attitudes that attack the person's own nature. Gluttony is a sin but not a crime. That is to say, the glutton diminishes his own gift of humanity by placing some gratification ahead of his duties and ahead of the higher call to serve God and man, but it does not constitute an attack on society or human rights. The church teaches forthrightly about the danger of gluttony, which is identified as one of the seven deadly sins. The state does not, however, make obesity crime.

Whenever we address a question of how a particular practice or action should rightly be treated in the law, therefore, it is necessary to bear in mind this distinction between crime and sin. There is a certain sort of society in which this distinction is suppressed. The common name for them is "theocracy," and the practitioners are identified as "puritans." Their premise is to place the state at the service of the moral law, and that appears at first blush to be a high-minded choice.

Everyone is somewhat familiar with the Christian Puritans of New England and absolutely everyone is familiar now with the Taliban regime of Afghanistan. The leaders of both of these states considered themselves to be paragons of righteousness who were simply doing their moral duty. We view them as dangerous fanatics who discarded the separation of church and state and who claimed to impose god's law on their unfortunate people. We are never called upon to supersede the Lord's judgements with our own judgement of right. We are all subject to his judgement and will answer for our lives—both for what we have done and for what we should have done but did not do—and he judges justly. No one of us judges justly and no one of us has he commissioned to make those decisions. This does not in any way diminish our duty to speak out on moral matters, and to condemn gluttony and obesity according to the example I used before, but it establishes that unless these sins are also crimes, we are not to invoke the police powers of the state to punish them.

Moral Judgment of Abortion

The moral consequence of elective abortion is not in doubt. The Catholic church has expressed herself unequivocally on the matter at all times, though some practical aspects which hinge on our growing understanding of gestation has evolved over time. In any case, the moral teaching on abortion has been unchanged in any way for about five hundred years and will not change substantially in the future. Elective abortion is the unjustified taking of innocent life and is tantamount to murder. Elective abortion is a sin of the gravest kind. The Catholic church and indeed all competent persons have both the right and the duty to proclaim and to defend this truth and to take all practical steps to educate the public and to defend innocent life. This is a personal moral duty, but the accompanying duty to take practical steps to defend innocent life inevitably raises abortion as a legal and civic matter. In what follows, accordingly, I will address two companion matters: how elective abortion should be approached in the law, and what the people can and should attempt to achieve within politics and the law in regard to abortion.

Legal Status of Abortion

In this discussion it will be necessary to disentangle two very different areas in which abortion arises before the law. One might style them "abortion in the narrow sense," and "issues raised by abortion." The narrow sense comprises the act of elective abortion itself. The latter category is by its nature elastic, as new issues arise repeatedly. I will refer to these topics as simply "abortion" and "ramifications," respectively.

Stated in its simplest terms, the pro-choice position on abortion is that whatever may be the morality of abortion, abortion is not a crime because it does not attack the fundamental human rights or the civil order. Like gluttony and avarice, it is simply not something that the law and the civil authorities are competent to control. No one has proposed a constitutional amendment denouncing jealousy, it might be said, and so why should there be an amendment dealing with elective abortion? From a moral perspective abortion is not more serious than avarice and uncontrollable jealousy. All are deadly sins, but it is not the function of the law to save people from themselves, or to save them from condemnation. It is only the task of the law to stop them from hurting each other.

There is some merit in this argument and it cannot by any means be dismissed out of hand. Everyone, including the Church, recognizes the cogency of the proposition at its most basic level. It is for that reason that the Church does not endorse drastic measures to prevent elective abortions from happening. Throughout the long centuries when abortion was illegal, many abortions nonetheless took place. In all that time, the Church repeatedly asserted the wrongness of abortion, but she did not appeal to the police to take harsh measures to prevent women from aborting their children. The Church recognized that was not and is not the proper job of the police. This is not to say that the Church or the law turned a blind eye to abortion. Far from it. In settings where it was feasible to prevent abortions, as for instance in ordinary hospitals, that was done. But the police did not, and were not urged to, execute widespread crackdowns in the hope of stopping abortion entirely. The legal treatment of abortion drifted in the same demi-monde of legal ambiguity as prostitution and the use of narcotics. That is not good, because abortion is a sin of the gravest kind, an almost unconscionable sin, but it is appropriate as a legal response and the Church and the general public endorsed it. It is not good, but it is better than to pervert the police powers of the state in a disruptive and—in the end—intolerable way. Individual abortions do not necessarily undermine the civil order as long as the moral judgement of abortion is clearly understood and widely supported.

This proposition surely smacks of polite hypocrisy, and it is. The civil law and civil society are littered with moral compromises and polite hypocrisy. It is not the moral judgement that is hypocritical. The moral judgement is clear. The compromises arise when the state gets involved, and have to do with what actual steps the law proposes to take in light of the morality. This is hypocrisy in a colloquial sense, but it is not moral hypocrisy. It is hypocrisy for a person to denounce drunkenness while himself a drunkard, or to condemn theft while he himself is a thief. It is not hypocrisy for one to denounce drunkenness or theft, but yet not to call out the dragoons to round up the drunkards and to dispose of the thieves summarily. Since the state does not make or enforce moral judgements—only the Lord our god does that—it is not hypocrisy to make different demands on the state and its laws than one places on personal behavior. Not only is this separation *not* hypocrisy, it is in reality justice, and its contrary is unjust Puritanism. More correctly stated, it is not hypocrisy the sin, it is "hypocrisy" the legal and social necessity.

The law tolerates sin because the alternative, which is a fanatical Taliban regime, would be a far greater injustice. It is an hypocritical compromise only to the extent that it is hypocritical of the state to let petty thieves off with less than life imprisonment or death.

The Direct Ramifications

Guilt is a thief that steals the conscience.

The reason that churches and other moral leaders teach and implore morality is that the immoral life brings with it guilt—real guilt as well as perceived guilt—that can become a fatal disease. Guilt becomes a disease when the reality of it becomes too frightening to confront, and the person retreats into denial and evasion. Guilt has at that point metastasized into a cancer that spreads throughout the whole person, and beyond him to everyone around him. The state can and should be restrained in its methods of suppressing elective abortion, but in the end the trail of guilt becomes a threat to the society which cannot be ignored.

There is a sense in which murder is the perfect, victimless crime. When did a victim ever come forward to level charges against the murderer or to testify in open court? The victim no longer matters. The victim whose interests we defend in a murder trial is the general public, who recognize that if murder was allowed to go unchecked they too would never be safe. That is to say, the victim is a victim not of the actual crime, but of hypothetical future crimes. This is another way of saying that crime, unlike sin, is an attack on the civil order and on human rights. In the case of elective abortion, then, we have to ask ourselves who are the victims and who is threatened by this practice. What we find is that it is environment of guilt which multiplies the harm and that attacks the community at large. For the moment, however, I will focus attention on victims who are close to the actual event.

One class of victims who are too easily forgotten is other, surviving children of the woman who has aborted one of her children. Can we suppose that they are not affected? Does their mother love them more than the unfortunate brother or sister, or were they just at the right place at the right time? I propose, and urge objective research on this question, that such children—wholly apart from whether they know the actual factual details—can ever have the same trust in their mother that children need to have in order to develop healthy self-respect. Certainly they are receiving the message that they do not have intrinsic moral worth; that they are not inherently valuable and lovable. They receive on the contrary the message that human life is not different from animal life, and that the gratifications of the day are the standard of worth. It is hardly a coincidence that we now see a so-called animal rights movement. Animals have no rights, and they never will because they are not capable of having rights. To equate us to the animals is not to confer rights on the animals, but to deny them to us. This is truly a Satanic cult that promotes such ideas, and more to the point it is a crime against the human society. It predicates precisely the attack on fundamental human rights which the state is instituted to defend.

Are there other proximate victims of elective abortion? I will not pursue this topic here but it needs further consideration.

The Indirect Ramification

Practitioners of elective abortion no longer want to escape, or even to be ignored. They now want exoneration and vindication. This need for vindication comes directly from the oppressive burden of guilt that the sin of abortion imposes on everyone who is associated with it.

One immediate target of the movement to vindicate abortion is modern medicine and the medical practice. Two areas are particularly topical today. One is an attempt to redefine medical education to include mandatory training in abortion practices. The other is related to it, and entails mandating abortion practice at all hospitals and clinics, and through all health insurance plans. The effect of the redefinition of medical training is to exclude persons who oppose abortion on moral grounds. This is not merely a matter of abortion. Its purpose is to marginalize a large fraction of society by excluding them from the practice of medicine. This campaign has had recent successes. The city of New York now specifies that all doctors who train in New York City—not only at public hospitals, but all hospitals—be trained in elective abortion. This ordinance comes of course from the city itself, and it amounts to state-sponsored discrimination against conscientious opponents of abortion. Just to make sure that the matter is clear and the record complete, I would point out that doctors who train in the city of New York are not obliged to study dentistry or psychiatry. No one doubts that these are legitimate medical specialties, but the ordinary physician is not expected to get trained in them. The practice of abortion is different and seemingly superior to them. The relevant point here is not one of the practice of medicine itself, of course, but the crime of discrimination against opponents of elective abortion.

The attack on hospitals and clinics is as widespread, if not more so. In the state of Illinois, all hospitals are now obliged by law to provide abortion counseling to victims of rape. The purpose and the effect of this law is to make it impossible for the Catholic church, which has run charitable hospitals for almost two millennia, to operate any hospital. At the present time—winter, 2002—the hierarchy of the church is in negotiations with the state seeking compromise that would permit them to continue to run their hospitals, but any such compromise will surely be controversial and temporary. The abortion lobby has the Catholic hospitals, and other like-minded hospitals, clearly in its sights. The abortionists have stalked their prey for decades, and the prey will in the end not escape the cross-hairs.

Both of these movements are intended and will have the effect of excluding a large part of the society—Catholics account for close to thirty percent of the population—from full participation in the society by excluding them from the practice of medicine.

The trail of guilt does not stop at these instances, but spreads itself widely throughout the society and no one escapes it. To rationalize abortion requires a rejection of the sanctity of conception and birth, and even a rejection of masculinity and femininity. I will not dwell on the personal consequences, on the sense of diminishment and rejection. I cannot speak knowledgeably about them. The consequences for the health of the society are in any case testimony enough. In country after country where this rejection of sexuality prevails—Western Europe, the U.S. to a degree, Japan, and others without doubt—the society itself is visibly undermined. The birth rate in those places is very low, and in many cases falls below the replacement rate. In the West, immigration has obscured the impending decline of the native population, but the native peoples must be and are acutely aware of what is happening: the replacement of these ancient peoples by alien immigrants. We do not hesitate to assert that a nation belongs to all of those who make their home there, regardless of where they originated. Indeed, the "native" peoples are by no means entirely native either.[2] Nonetheless, the death of a people is a kind of poignant passing that can only evoke in us a sense of the heartbreak and despair that go with it.

So powerful is the sense of loss and the grief it causes that the people are now being offered as a substitute a false hope of artificial insemination and even so-called "cloning." the harm that will result from the belief that we can manufacture new men and women can hardly be overestimated. The philosopher Aldous Huxley saw this scandal for what it is, and so does every petty despot who eagerly sends his legions to their death, confident in the knowledge that he can always make more.

Conclusion

People of good will disagree from time to time about how exactly the Church and the state should best tackle their distinct missions. No one can presume to prejudge particular matters that will arise throughout history. The principles remain the same but the details of their application adapt to the time and the circumstances. One of those unchanging principles, however, has come under attack in modern times, and the resulting confusion can be very harmful. This confusion has to do with what are the rights that the state is ordained to defend. We understand that human rights are an unqualified gift from the Lord our god, who fashioned the human person in his own image and likeness. The state is a social construct created to defend and to enhance that gift of inalienable rights.

These human rights are general propositions, defined in rather broad terms and defined largely in terms not of legal relationships but of goals and intentions. It is the province of the state to apply them to particular circumstances, and in the process to create actionable rights: i.e., rights that are recognizable by a court of law. It may seem that since the court and the legal code are fashioned by the state, the state is the ultimate and true source of the rights themselves, but that is not true. The state is a servant of the people, who are the owners of their inalienable rights. It is not the master of the people, nor is it the source of those rights.

This is an important point in the context of the abortion debate, and proponents of abortion and their allies frequently distort it. In regard to the unborn child, his or her rights are defined by his or her person, without regard or reference to what the state is willing to do. As the state does not have the power to extinguish fundamental human rights, it does not have the power to create then. The state has the duty to manage the affairs of the society in the most prudent way, even if to do so it subordinates the rights of some persons, but it does not have the power to dissolve those rights. It can, in effect, decide that under certain circumstances elective abortion is not a crime, but it does not have the power to rule that abortion is not a sin and an invasion of the human rights of the child.

The same point has to be made on the opposite side of the debate, in regard to so-called animal rights. As the state does not have the power to extinguish rights, neither does it have the power to create rights where there are none. Animals have no fundamental human rights. Confusion about the source of our rights can be the cause of great mischief it is taken to mean that human rights are the creation of the state and are subject to it, to be created or destroyed at the whim of the law. That very clearly is a formula for unlimited tyranny and for the complete denial of our rights. It was for this reason, of course, that in the Declaration of Independence Thomas Jefferson clearly and unequivocally tied the actions of the colonies to the grant of inalienable rights which descend from our creator, in defiance of the wishes of the established authority in London.

This point recurs again in American history, in a dispute that resounds stirringly today. There is a very poignant parallel between elective abortion and slavery. This nation tolerated slavery for nearly a century before the contradictions, the injustices, that it brought forced a final violent resolution. For those ante-bellum decades, the hope persisted that slavery might remain a personal matter, a sort of victimless crime—if we blind ourselves to the rights of the enslaved persons—which could coexist peacefully with the free society. That proved to be a vain hope. The ramifications of slavery created a growing intrusion of crimes, of attacks on society and on the rights of all persons, that became intolerable. In the end, the judgement of the nation was the words spoken by her president, Abraham Lincoln: "A nation cannot live half slave and half free." To this truth we need now to add a second article.

A nation cannot survive with this contradiction running down the middle of her laws that the citizens have moral worth that is their birthright, and yet they are no better than and no different from the animals.

There is no state amongst the animals and there is no law or justice, because there is no society and no fundamental rights. To reject the spiritual nature of man, to reject his moral worth, does not glorify the state, it demolishes it. It is right and necessary to separate church and state, but it is impossible and preposterous to separate the state and justice.

Notes

1. My focus in these remarks is on the Catholic church because it is the church that is uniquely the source of the doctrine of separation. Of the many other religious institutions in the world, very few espouse such a doctrine, but that does not exempt them from it. Beyond that truism, there is very little that I can say about

their relations with the state.

The first government that I am aware of in the English-speaking world to commit itself to separation was the Maryland colony, which had been founded by Irish Catholic aristocrats. At the behest of Cecil Calvert, Lord Baltimore, the legislature promulgated an edict of religious tolerance and separation of church and state in 1649, in order to head off conflict with what we would now call "Fundamentalist" Christians. See the Maryland Toleration Act, in Henry Steele Commager, *Documents of American History.* 6th ed. (Appleton-Century-Crofts: New York, 1958).

2. The people of Central and Western Europe seem to be a merger of two types: truly aboriginal peoples—the blond and red-haired natives—and invading Celts and Slavs who came from what is now India. True is the Irish proverb that there are no pure races.

7

Freedom and Liberty and the Politics of Puritanism

The Declaration of Independence asserts for all persons an inalienable right to liberty. This is one of the greatest insights in all of political history, but what is inalienable is not, unfortunately, inevitable. It is always timely to rethink what Thomas Jefferson said on our behalf, his declaration broadcast to the whole world of the premise of the American nation.

We routinely use the words "freedom" and "liberty" interchangeably. Liberty is political freedom, and that is the topic of this essay, but there is much more to freedom. Freedom is a personal trait that is synonymous with free will. It is synonymous with a life lived under conscious self-direction. It is considered to be a truism, or nearly so, that we human beings have been endowed with free will by the gift of our human nature. That is not however strictly correct. We have been fashioned with both a desire and a capacity for free will. We call our will "free" because first of all no one else can literally force us to do what we do not want to do. They can only make far more pleasant to do what they want of us than to do what we want. We have been endowed with the capacity to weigh the true worth of all things and thus to choose whatever is good and to reject whatever is evil. We moreover wish to see ourselves in this light; to see ourselves as exercising free will. And we are responsible for how we use our will. The will with which we were born is not however free, even though it is capable of freedom.

It would be more accurate to describe our endowment as *autonomous will.* We have from birth the capacity to formulate demands and commands, to choose amongst alternatives and to devise plans to get what we want. These are all marks of autonomous will. The final step, the step from autonomy—control—to freedom is the capacity to reject folly and to choose good. We all have the will to gorge ourselves on junk food, but not everyone has the freedom to choose not to.

In summary, we are all willful people, but we are not all free people. If we were all free, political freedom—liberty—would be an automatic by-product and there would be nothing to talk about. But in this world liberty needs constantly to be reaffirmed and recreated because neither we nor any of our neighbors is entirely free. We honor those who are very free—who possess a well developed capacity to judge what is good and beneficial and to act on that judgement—but no one is completely free. Life and the world are filled with temptations. As we define the political context of liberty and the legal institutions that support it, therefore it is necessary to plan for and aim for a working liberty for people who are by no means completely free. Liberty, the political institution, is not the same as liberty the human right. It is the human right that our legal and political organizations serve and that justifies them, even in the presence of myriad compromises and approximations in practice. The political institutions of liberty cannot be justified except as they serve human liberty, but imperfection is inevitable and does not by itself invalidate the reality.

The urge to Puritanism in society arises from an unwillingness to let practical liberty get in the way of the perceived good. The same could be said of nearly any law. We must therefore look elsewhere to find guides that clarify the difference between laws that promote the common good and those that we would deem puritanical.

Three Denotations of Liberty

One obstacle that blocks the clarity we seek is ambiguity about what is meant by liberty. Everyone thinks he knows what he means by it, without being aware that other people attach quite different meanings. Very often, moreover, we settle for limited, casual connotations rather than demanding a complete definition.

Liberty as Equality

When we speak of liberty we often mean a demand for equal respect. We are very inclined to adopt this attitude, and we say something like, "I'm as good as the next man. No one can tell me what to do!" This is a legitimate consequence of liberty because it points to the companion virtue of responsibility. There is no freedom of any kind without responsibility. Freedom, which means acting out of conscious choice, cannot exist without personal responsibility. It is meaningless without the companion responsibility. To the extent therefore that liberty is understood as taking responsibility, it is valid.

Liberty as Efficiency

We sometimes use liberty to describe a relationship between people which promotes efficiency. The king decrees that in the interests of national unity, a highway be laid between cities A and B. To implement that decree, the government interviews makers of roads and bridges, and chooses one of them to be the general contractor for the project. At that point the government rests, authorizing the builder to carry out his plans and to deliver the finished highway as it is described in his proposal. The counselors do not kibbitz his work. The king does not second-guess his directions to the workers. It would be inefficient for all of those people, whose mission is the government of the realm, to try to replace the contractor whom they have hired in the day-to-day management of the job. They give him the liberty to implement their goals in his way.

This is not as familiar an interpretation of liberty as was my first example, but it is a very old and respectable one. The philosopher Leibniz asked, long ago, if the bird was free to fly and the fish free to swim. Answering from the position that liberty is equality, we might be tempted to say, "No, the bird is only free if it does not have to fly, and the fish free as long as it does not have to swim." Leibniz's answer, however, was the opposite. The bird has a particular nature: it was fashioned to fly, and the fish was made to swim. Therefore, to fly is freedom for the bird and to swim is freedom for the fish. It would be a denial of their freedom to prevent them from doing what they were made to do. These creatures are happy when they are allowed to do what they were made to do, and it is what they would choose. This is a very deep insight into freedom. If freedom is the ability to make good choices, even hard ones, then it presumes a scale of values in which some choices are intrinsically good and other intrinsically wrong.

From these partial definitions we find that liberty is a good in and for itself—something that promotes other goods—for two reasons. First, it diminishes conflict among people by respecting their individual dignity. Human beings naturally resist intrusions on their autonomy, impositions of external tyranny, because they need and value a recognition of their individual worth. Secondly, liberty is good because it frees people to seek and to do what is good for them. No one is privileged to know exactly what he should do today. There is no kind of science as detailed as that. He has to be allowed to find it out for him- or herself. When we speak of the political right of liberty, however, we need to connect these ideas with the nature and constitution of the state.

Liberty as Limited Government

Our liberty, our political freedom, rests on twin pillars. The first of them is the truth that the state exists to serve us, and not the other way around. The other pillar is that the state, like any institution, has limited capabilities. There are only certain things that it does well. In order to serve us, it must recognize its limitations and accept them. The American nation was founded on a recognition of the limitations of the state, but gradually over time the state has grown beyond the bounds of its commission. It was a malicious weed that flourished in the nineteenth century and that flowered in the crazed "isms" of the twentieth century that threw off the wraps, threw off the limitations of the state and ushered in the totalitarian state.

In the *Preface* to this book I promised to apply conservative philosophy to the law and to the state, which I will continue to do. The totalitarian state is, however, an offense against the progressive philosophy as well. It is at home only with fascism. The progressive premise—also called "Liberalism"—means that to the highest degree possible the people be left free to do whatever they want. The progressive or liberal case for limited government is therefore grounded directly on the right of liberty. For the state to expand its authority at the expense of the liberty of the people is a direct violation of the highest purpose of the state itself. As far as it goes, this is an acceptable conservative position as well. What conservatism adds is the proposition that the correct functions of the state are derived from fundamental truths. When the state oversteps its bounds, we can do more than simply protest and resist because it infringes our liberty. We can rethink the proper role of the state, and work to return it to the things it should be concerned with.

In Catholic philosophy—so deeply conservative, of course—this doctrine of limited government is expressed in the doctrine of *subsidiarity*.[1] That doctrine has two propositions. First, viewing the hierarchy of social institutions, from the individual person to the governments of nations and of the world, the responsibility and authority for all decisions should be allocated to the smallest—the most personal—level that is competent to make it. Where the person is capable of deciding, it is his or her choice. If he or she is not capable, the responsibility naturally ascends to the family. Where the family is also not able, to the community, and so on.

The second proposition is clearly related to the first.

It is that the state should only do what the people are unable to do for themselves. George Stigler offered an amendment, which is that the state should only do what it does well. Both propositions obtain. The state should do only what the people and their other institutions cannot do for themselves, and even with this restriction, it should not undertake anything that it can not arguably do well. When the state undertakes some task, it changes the relationship between the state and the community, because it spreads its monopoly of power that inevitably expands beyond the scope of its new responsibilities. If, moreover, it should fail to do what it undertakes, the state is very disinclined to seek correction and to back down from its lofty claims. Far more often it begins to devise excuses and cover to hide its mistakes. The great importance of the jobs given to the state and the deep legitimacy accorded to its commands and to its leaders are used as an excuse to hide failure, on the grounds that they might undermine the loyalty of the people. This is, in fact, the plot of Shakespeare's *MacBeth*. A little failure can become the father of widespread and systemic abuse of power. So at the very least, the state should not undertake any task at which it is highly likely to fail, even if it seems otherwise to be a justifiable assumption of authority.

The American government has apparently taken it upon itself to bring democracy to the whole world. This seems to me an undertaking at which they will almost surely fail. The world is too big to be pushed around, and the people of the world are much too likely to think that falling into the line drawn by Washington is not only *not* democracy, it is actually the *opposite* of democracy. They tend to think that democracy means their governments doing what their people want them to do, not what we want them to do.

The right to liberty rests on the recognition of the essentially limited powers and authority of the state, and of all the various institutions that exist under the state. These limitations were at one time defined by the terms of the American Constitution. Over the years, however, the bonds that maintained those limitations have been loosened, and the national government is today very little hindered from any undertaking and from claiming any power that it pleases. Too little thought has been given along the way to the question of what the government should do; and its mission is and what it is able to do in reality. As a result it has been given tasks for which it cannot in fact be responsible, to achieve results that it cannot in fact accomplish. It is the right of liberty that suffers. Although we can see violations of limited government in our own land, the desire to claim irresponsible power is by no means a uniquely American trait.

The greatest and most outrageous claims being made today for illegitimate powers are the presumptions of the Taliban, whose thesis is that the government—a certain kind of Islamist government—can bring about the reign of truth and justice as it subjects everyone to the rules of Shari'a. Shari'a, which is usually translated as "Islamic law," is actually broader than "law" as we understand that term. It encompasses not only laws, but also a broader way of life under divine guidance. It is the Islamic way of life, and according to the Taliban it delivers the promise of heaven on Earth. But there is no heaven on Earth. There is no perfection on Earth. Whether or not one avers that there is a place where god alone rules, we can all agree that this planet is not that place. Anyone who promises a heaven on Earth is planning a Hell of a heaven for us poor mortals who are going to have to live there. The urge that gives rise to Taliban is not confined to any religious creed or to any race or nationality. It arises everywhere and amongst all people. I call it the "urge to puritanism."

Modern American Puritanism

It would be nearly impossible not to notice how many people are on a campaign to put in place some new rule of law, usually one designed to change the way you live. Seat belts, fifty-five-mile speed limits, and now PETA all want to make some changes. The merits of any particular campaign have to be debated in terms of what is being proposed. The proposal to make everyone wear a seat belt while riding in a car, for instance, needs to be investigated and debated in terms of highway safety and convenience, and the cost both of implementing seat belts and of enforcing this dictate. The personalities involved in any single issue are not relevant; to mix personal attacks into debate is the time-worn fallacy of *argumentum ad hominem*.

Whether we should all wear seat belts and whether animals are capable of having human rights have to be studied and reasoned through without regard to whether or not the proponents of seat belts are invasive nags or the opponents of animal rights are insensitive chauvinists. Campaigns of these sorts arise in our country for a reason, however, and it is both legitimate and necessary to stop a while to consider why they arise. What is it that causes small groups of highly committed people to latch onto one cause or another and to make it a sort of crusade? We have a legitimate need to understand what causes important social phenomena of all kinds, and what to make of those causes.

One possible explanation presents itself immediately. Perhaps everyone really should wear a seat belt at all times, and perhaps animals really do have human rights—or more correctly, maybe we really do have only animal rights. One explanation for such campaigns is that they are right, and as so often happens in life at the start only a few persons have correctly thought through the issues. The same could be said for prohibition and the evils of drink—presumably including red wine—and vegetarianism and the evils of eating meat, and of many other practices that have endured the opprobrium of vigilant reformers. It would be both foolish and unnecessary, moreover, to say that none of the programs of this sort has merit. I do not, however, think that the abundance of such moralistic campaigns has anything to do with their individual merits. I think it has to do with the perceived rewards of campaigning as an end in itself, and it is that thesis that I intend to explore.

The Urge to Puritanism

I'm sure that it has not escaped anyone's attention how nice it is to be able to tell other people what they should and should not do. Nothing could be more affirming of one's own worth than to be accorded the power to dictate to other, perhaps wayward, persons. As a general proposition that could hardly be denied. It explains for instance why persons are so willing, and even eager, to be kings and queens, or better yet emperors and empresses. Along with a royal crown goes a kind of certificate of authenticity, and those who wear the crown bask in the legitimacy that their subjects confer to them. Universal recognition is, however, not easy to create. Claims of authority are more likely to arouse resistance and hostility than willing compliance unless there is some agreed upon standard of authority and source of legitimacy. Every religion has produced puritanical movements which appeal not to earthly crowns, but to divine Providence to ratify their authority. The Puritans of colonial New England and the Wahhabis of modern Arabia are familiar examples. While in the end every such movement has foundered and eventually disappeared, they often persist for a century or more. It seems therefore that divine legitimacy is an effective formula for public acceptance.

In today's secular societies, appeal to divine Providence is not available because there is no consensus on whether there is a god or, even granting that point, who he is. Secularism introduces, in this regard, something equivalent to polytheism, in which each person chooses, or defines, his or her own god. Any appeal to any one of these gods may be effective for like-minded devotees but the majority of the community is unmoved and indifferent. We are therefore left with this situation. A large number of the citizens wish to have an impact on the society as a whole, to make rules that others must bend to. There is, however, no mechanism to do this, except for a very small elite who hold high office. It is interesting, by the way, how much more attractive state office has become for the ambitious, and in particular how much a preferred path the state capital has become in comparison to national office. The difference between a governor and a senator is that the governor has personal authority while the senator has none—or seems to have none, because we do not know what actually goes on in the proverbial corridors of power. Thus the state house draws those who wish to wield authority.

To summarize, democratic society promises to empower all those citizens who desire to have a visible impact on society, but evidently it does not actually provide enough offices which deliver that power.

The Role of Political Entrepreneurship

There are many ways to establish links of cooperation and loyalty in a democratic polity. Most often, it seems, the basis is ethnic, and that in turn takes two possible forms: tribal and religious. In the U.S. today this however explains only a part of our political demography. The Black Power movement, led ultimately by Jesse Jackson, and the Religious Right, identified principally with Jerry Falwell and Pat Robertson, are obvious examples. These leaders are, in turn, political entrepreneurs who set out to create a "public"—this was the term coined by social democrats—around the propositions and the programs of action to make it the law of the land. In outline, the appeals are quite similar. The syllogism runs:

We agree that the public would be better off if they _____.
It is our ardent desire, and the desire of all public servants, to make the public better off. Therefore, Q.E.D., the public should be required to _____.

There is a lot wrong with this declaration. First of all, in a democracy it is up to the public as a whole to decide what would make them better off. It is not the job of the minority to force them to be better, even if we grant the wisdom of the minority. It is furthermore not the commission of public servants to make the public better. It is their commission to do their job, confident in the belief that what they do makes the public better off. And confident, moreover, in the recognition that if what they do violates the limited constitution of the state, it will do little to make the public better off and is very likely to make them worse off.

Notes

1. The basis for this rather obscure term is that idea that the higher institutions are subsidiary to the lower, more particular ones. All rights and all needs are defined first of all in terms of the person. The family has then subsidiary rights and duties deriving from the members, the community has subsidiary rights and duties deriving from the people and from the family, and so on up the line.

Part Three

On Divorce

8

The Divorce Economy:
A Pragmatic View of Divorce
in Society

Moses permitted you to divorce because of the hardness of your hearts, but I tell you this. There is no divorce. Whom god has joined let no man rend asunder.

—Jesus of Nazareth

Divorce is rarely discussed in polite society. It happens, and happens with ever-increasing frequency, but it is not suitable for discussion. I do not, of course, purpose to consider the practical aspects of getting divorced, because they are covered at great length in the law. By the same token I do not propose to treat the personal experience of divorce. That is a subject on which I am not by any means an expert, and on which I suspect very few persons are expert. In any case, it is the aspect of divorce that gets repeated airing in the popular theater and in the press and the literature of the people. Whether these sources deal with realities or with myth I do not propose to judge, leaving that to persons more expert than I. What I do intend to consider here is what the institution of divorce means in a social context. How it shapes and is shaped by all the other realities of social organization. This is a broad topic, and one about which I have only a little of value to offer. Any thoughtful reader will, under the best of circumstances, come away from reading this short essay inspired by a desire to know more about these matters, and perhaps wondering if he has learned anything here, and if what I have to say will in the end hold up to scrutiny. That is as it should be.

The term "divorce" was historically limited to separation on account of adultery. Other acts of separation of husband and wife were referred to as "renunciation." Among modern people, there is no such distinction drawn, and both are called divorce. I will follow the modern usage, by which divorce is an legal ending of a marriage and marital rights and duties.

The Simple Economics of Divorce

Every divorce is accompanied by detailed and often acrimonious parceling out of the common property. Divorce law is, in fact, a branch of property law, and except for providing for any dependent children, the whole proceeding is preoccupied with the division of assets and with claims on income. As a result, the finances of divorced women have rightly been the subject of very thorough study. The focal point of these studies is the individual person, generally the former wife. Too little attention is paid to the social dimension of economics of divorce, which is my topic in this section. When focusing on the individuals, the issues are psychological and perhaps moral. The social implications are, however, social science, and it is the perspective of a social science that I plan to adopt. Inherent in a social science, we do not propose that what results is an accurate picture of any single case because our method is to generalize and to extract common features that are found in many particular cases. The proof or disproof of the social sciences is, therefore, inherently statistical and deals with representative archetypes because individual exceptions, while they do point to limitations of the study, do not invalidate it.

Divorce in America today is not merely a personal act. It is for everyone a defining element of the social milieu. No one is untouched by divorce. The great majority of the population have some rather firsthand knowledge of it, either in their own divorce or that of their parents or of their children. Each of these persons is affected directly by the divorce of friends or family. More important however is the impact of this milieu on expectations. Every person who is at all aware of current social norms has to adjust his or her expectations in light of the high probability of divorce, and must adjust the way he or she raises his or her own children in light of the high probability that they also will end up in divorce. The only exception to this would be small slices of society that exist in tight-knit subcultures immune to the forces of the broader society. There are some persons of this type, and I will return to that interesting topic later, but almost by definition these are the exception and account for only a small fraction of the population. The large majority of the people must rationally adjust both their own expectations and their expectations and plans for their children in light of the high probability of divorce. In this section I intend to trace out the consequences of those adjustments in rather simple financial terms.

The nature of marriage is partnership between man and woman in which each helps the partner and both help their children by applying their particular talents and inclinations. Men help their wives and women help their husbands, though they do so in very different ways. Similarly, both help their children, although here again their help is expressed or realized in very different ways. To put it in a nutshell, husbands do what they do best and wives do what they do best. The children happily absorb all of this attention, which is what children do best.

The result of this partnership is that neither husband nor wife is self-sufficient. Each is capable of surviving on his or her own. They are not so interdependent as to lose that capacity, but neither one can singlehandedly achieve the way of life that they create together. In this sense they are interdependent. The culture of divorce attacks that interdependence in a radical way. Any benefit or value that depends on the partnership can vanish in an instant. That is of course obvious to everyone where we are speaking *ex post,* describing a particular couple who divorce. The social consequences however come from the expectation of divorce and not from the outcome of any particular event by itself. The vast majority of men and women, when they contemplate marriage and when they prepare for life, must anticipate the outcomes of divorce and must be prepared for the defeasibility of the marital partnership. They can still enter some sort of marriage, but the marriage they enter is radically different from the conventional idyll. These are the generalities of the case, but now I wish to plunge into a specific, stylized example which will convey much better than dry precepts the nature of the adjustment.

In marriage the woman depends on her spouse for material goods that they and their children need. Quite obviously that dependence is a very risky proposition when the husband can simply walk away and take his income with him. A young woman, then has to prepare to support herself financially because her husband's promise to do so is not a credible promise. It may be heartfelt and may even hold up over the course of a long married life, but it is not enforceable at law and is therefore not credible in advance. The woman's recourse is to her own ability to earn a living.

So consider the case of a young wife and mother, well educated and practical. Her husband, also well educated, has a steady job that pays a very respectable $100,000. They could live on that sum, paying roughly $30,000 in income taxes and living with their two children on the remaining $70,000. Now suppose that this young woman begins to doubt her husband's faithfulness. As explained above, the villain in this piece is actually expectations that she would have formed long before, but for the purposes of this scenario I will assume that up until this moment she had been blissfully unaware of the risk of divorce.

Thanks to her fine education, she is able to land a job that pays $75,000 per year. Because of the progressive nature of the income tax, she pays a 40 percent tax rate, which leaves her with $45,000 after tax. She also now needs someone to look after the children. That costs $24,000 per year, and these are after-tax dollars. This leaves $21,000 from her salary. The nanny owes her own taxes, by the way, which take about $4,000 in social security tax. If the nanny is married, her taxes are probably larger because they are based on the family income, but in fact most nannies are unmarried.

So, to sum up the figures as they stand to this point, of the additional income of $75,000, the woman and her family keep $21,000, and nanny keeps $20,000, and the government keeps $34,000. Aside from the dollars and cents of income, there are several adjustments that I will not attempt to quantify. First, her job entails direct expenses. Conceivably they could take most of the $21,000. The woman is not really working for the money that she brings into this family, and so she would if necessary be willing to spend all her newfound income on expenses of the job. She is working to prepare for the day when she will have to support herself. If that arises, her taxes will be lower, her salary may very well have been raised, and in any case she can then start to conserve on expenses if she has to. As long as she and her husband are sharing their combined income, there is no need for her to scrimp. However I do not assume that she spends the whole $21,000. It is more plausible that she actually adds to the net household income.

The other adjustments are not quantified in terms of money value. On the one hand, she has the unpleasant knowledge that her children are being raised by the hired help. This is something that mothers find to be very vexing, as they freely admit in countless interviews and surveys. Over against that, she has the satisfactions of her job, net of the diminished satisfaction of her household occupation. Economics is not only about money, but I do not intend to try to weigh these costs and benefits. That they are real is obvious to every reader.

We cannot stop the scenario at this point, however. The implications for the husband need also to be considered because this is a comprehensive accounting of a typical family, and not just of a typical wife. Marriage is a partnership in which man and woman help each other in the ways that they are best at. Because this analysis is narrowly economic, I have fixed on the husband's contribution to his family's material well-being, although this is by no means his only contribution. In any case, what economic contribution does a wife make to her husband? Her chief contribution of that sort is to support his work, by

138

encouragement and advice when needed. The husband in my scenario earns $100,000 doing the work for which he prepared himself at school and by earlier experience. His income is by no means a given, however, nor is it the result of his effort alone. He could not do that job without help from his wife.

Now, let us back up a bit in the script and make one change. We had assumed that the wife never anticipated the day when she would have to support herself, but that is unrealistic. Quite the contrary, even before she started to prepare for her own career, her parents had begun to prepare her. As a result, this young lady has much less incentive to invest in her own husband's career, and should redirect her investment at her own. What results when she does not invest in her husband's income potential? He does not receive the support that he needs and the investment that he needs. Thus, whereas he could hypothetically have held down a job to earn $100,000, he must in fact settle for a more modest career and a salary of $70,000.

Let us again add up the figures. In an ideal world, the husband would earn $100,000 pre-tax, and the family would live on the $70,000 of after-tax income. In the divorce society, husband and wife have combined income of $145,000. From this they pay $58,000[1] of taxes and also lay out $24,000 for the nanny. That leaves them with $63,000 to live on. They actually have lost $7,000, and this is before netting off the wife's job expenses!

As these rough, indicative figures make clear, divorce is a terrible deal from a purely financial perspective. It is enormously costly for this man and woman. The cause of the loss is the loss of the wife's investment in her husband's income. From a purely economic calculation she could in theory earn a higher return on her time and talents by raising her husband's income than she can by trying to replace it. That is not in any way to impugn her intelligence or character. It is only, rather, to apply the law of comparative advantage. The most valuable activity she could pursue, from a purely financial point of view, is to invest in her husband's income. The expectation of divorce, or what I am calling here the divorce society, makes that potentially a foolish commitment.

These purely financial relationships have personal consequences too. Marriage is partnership in which wife and husband share their income. The expectation of divorce, or what I am calling here the divorce society, makes that potentially a foolish commitment.

These purely financial relationships have personal consequences too. Marriage is partnership in which wife and husband help each other. The expectation of divorce discourages both husband and wife from helping each other. What really happens when we defeat the conventional marital relationship?

The husband entered into marriage to find in his wife a woman who could invest in his prospects, and who would make him more successful than he could be on his own. His wary wife, however, cannot do that. So his hopes and desires are defeated. He becomes disillusioned and angry that his wife has failed him.

The wife enters marriage to find a man who could relieve her of the burden of making a living, which would free her to do what she does best. The divorce society has however prevented her from trusting that her husband will actually do that, and so she is forced to provide for herself, or at least to prepare to provide for herself. Instead of the comfortable income of $100,000 that she could reasonably have expected her rather promising husband to earn, she finds that the bum settles for a dead-end job that pays only $70,000. It is obvious to her that he has turned out to be lazy and lacking in ambition. She is thankful to have her own career, although it is second-best.

Thus the husband resents his wife because she cannot or will not help him to achieve what he wants and what he knows he could achieve, and the wife resents her husband because he does not even try to support his family as he should. They are well on their way to divorce. In this simple and highly practical example we see at work the essential dynamic of the divorce society: Divorce as a social institution makes it difficult if not impossible for a man and woman to marry. Oversimplifying for effect, it could almost be said that to legalize divorce is to outlaw marriage! Which is the greater freedom? To be permitted to divorce or to be permitted to marry?

The Legal Institution of Divorce: The Divorce Industry

As a second line of investigation, I plan to look more closely into the legal environment of divorce. That is to say, to look into both the terms of divorce law and the roles of the many parties to the institution of divorce—attorneys, courts, counselors, and so on. Again, my method is the method of social sciences, which require that I ask *why* these arrangements exist in the form in which they exist and to ask *what* is the actual result that they produce.

The legal institutions of divorce are in every respect an industry, as usually defined in economics. It is an industry in the same way that medical care is an industry that serves paying customers. Because the central institution of this industry is the court of law, it is assumed that the process is one of adjudicating conflicts as an impartial referee, but that is not all how the divorce industry actually operates. It is in effect a promoter of its product, which is divorce settlements, and it is geared to enlarge its own importance in every way possible.

The aggregate revenues of the divorce industry are very large. Most are paid directly out of the wealth of the combatant parties, though the state and other public or quasi-public institutions contribute as well. The young, aspiring professor of family law is a case in point. She, by her scholarship and by what she teaches, helps to formulate the law. To the extent that her thoughts are amenable to the divorce bar at large, she will be rewarded with a seat on the divorce bench, so her incentive is clearly to shape the law in a way that the bar finds convenient. Once settled on the bench, this young judge decides according to the rules of law as she knows them and has taught them. What she says is the law. The losing party could appeal, but the process of appeal is largely irrelevant for two reasons. First of all, few parties to divorce are inclined to add further to their legal costs by appealing, and secondly the justices of appeal are simply other trial judges who have been promoted up the line. The result is that there is no disinterested review and rethinking of the law of divorce by persons whose livelihood does not come from the system as it exists today.

The really big money in this industry, however, is earned by those who deal directly with the customer, or in other words, by the divorce bar. They are in the position of being paid very well for every divorce decree that is issued, and not being paid, or paid very little at all, for every one that is not issued. They are paid in proportion to the number of divorces that they bring about. They are paid to cause divorce. The best test of whether, or to what extent, the divorce bar succumbs to this incentive would be the proportion of cases in which a married couple initially approached attorneys, but subsequently renewed their marriage and did not divorce. I would venture that especially in recent times this number is only a tiny fraction as large as the number of divorces, but in any case the facts will not lie.

The underlying reason for this perverse incentive is that the focal point of the divorce is the division of joint assets and the negotiating of claims on future income. The value that an attorney adds, therefore, lies in representing his party in this allocation, and naturally then the remuneration of the attorney is based on his or her success. If there is no division of the property, there is no basis for measuring success or failure, and in any case the contribution of the attorney is small. In that case, a small fixed fee is appropriate. As the attorney's contribution lies in dividing the property, it is necessary to actually divide the property to make that contribution. On the other hand, the clientele have not approached lawyers in order to stay married. They would not need lawyers for that purpose, and they have no reason whatever to reward their counsel for bringing about a reconciliation. That is not to say that the parties are initially set on divorce. Rather, it is only to say that that is not the service that they are purchasing from the attorney. They pay the attorney to bring about a divorce, and they pay him or her for representing their financial interests in the division of the common assets.

The perverse financial incentives do not simply rest with the attorneys however. More to the point, the attorneys are not simply passive providers of this service. In addition to the court and the bar, there is a third profession that contributes to the divorce industry, and they are the marriage counselors. It is here that the financial incentives are most clearly pivotal.

Persons who approach a marriage counselor are, like persons who approach a doctor or any other professional, uninformed about what they want and about what the future holds. That is true of a medical patient pondering major surgery for himself, but it is even truer of a person whose complaint is in his or her marriage. In that case, the "problem" is with another person. The client is almost entirely at the mercy of the counselor because the counselor, on account of his unique role, is the one who claims to actually know what is going on and what the future is likely to bring. As with the divorce bar, the best test of what marriage counselors actually accomplish would be the results, in terms of what fraction of their clients are reconciled and what fraction proceed to divorce. I would rather confidently assert that very few reconcile and nearly all divorce.

The reason for the apparent lack of success of the counseling profession—the infrequency with which they achieve a reconciliation—is in part the public acceptance of divorce. Reconciliation is not generally viewed as being even an appropriate goal of counseling, because divorce is viewed as normal and healthy. The more immediate reason, however, is again financial. The divorce bar has every incentive to use marriage counselors to generate business for themselves. It is only natural for a marriage counselor and a divorce lawyer to work together, sharing the revenues generated by divorce. The counselor has presumably the trust of one of the parties. That is why that party sought him out in the first place, to be an advisor and a repository of trust. The counselor's advice on legal counsel is an integral part of the service he or she performs, to which the client would have to place a high value. Thus the marriage counselor functions as a broker between candidates for divorce, on the one hand, and the divorce bar on the other. This is a very normal business development function, for which the divorce lawyer would be willing to pay. The perverse financial incentive that motivates the attorney is therefore transferred to the marriage counselor. The counselor in turn has both the opportunity and the incentive to cause his clients to divorce.

These three classes of persons—the judges, and divorce attorneys, and the marriage counselors—comprise all who are actually employed in the divorce industry, but they are not the whole industry. Divorce and divorce law exist in a broader environment of law and of popular culture. This context his highly similar to the social context of, for instance, the tobacco industry. The parties with a direct stake in promoting tobacco and in promoting divorce have no natural counterweight. There is no anti-smoking industry and there is no contra-divorce industry either.

The law of divorce is created bit by bit, like most law, from cases decided by divorce courts, as codified and rationalized by legal scholars. This is the benchmark that is presented to both the general courts of appeal and to the legislature. The question that they actually address is not "what should be the law of divorce?" but rather "why should we change this prevailing law?" It is by no means impossible that they would want to force some change, but that is not going to happen in the natural course of events. In terms of my analogy, there may be an anti-smoking movement, but there is no anti-smoking industry. The intellectual resources of the divorce law—faculty at law schools, sitting judges, and legislators—are first of all drawn from the ranks of the industry itself and have no reason to harbor great reformist zeal. Anyone who does happen to desire radical change is, moreover, most unlikely to rise far in this world since he or she is antagonistic to the interests of all the existing participants.

The marriage counseling profession contributes also to the maintenance of this intellectual environment, by promoting the idea that divorce is natural and normal, and that the denial of divorce is both an intrusion on a person's freedom and is a danger to his or her health and happiness. As with the rules of the law, there is no other source of information about divorce than the thoughts of the counselors, who are a self-selected group of presumed experts. Indeed, they are expert in the narrow sense that they possess a unique body of relevant evidence. They do not have an incentive to analyze and generalize from this experience in a disinterested way, however, because they are employed in the industry. They are, in this context, what are commonly known as "hired guns."

This is not very different from appointing plastic surgeons to promulgate standards of facial beauty. We can be fairly sure that in the gaze of plastic surgeons beauty rarely occurs spontaneously and by unassisted chance in nature.

The divorce industry, in sum, is a rather self-contained and self-justifying enterprise which operates largely without any objective review. It is a very profitable industry, supporting the livelihood of many thousands of persons, many of whom make a very comfortable living. It would be interesting to attach some actual numbers to this: to determine how many divorce lawyers there are and what is their aggregate income, for instance.

I am not in any sense proposing an intrusive accounting of this, but only the sort of rough estimate that could be obtained from court records and from a knowledge of what are the usual fee arrangements. What is needed here is nothing like an exact accounting, because this is all perfectly legitimate income of the divorce bar, but some reasonable estimate of how large is this endeavor in relation to, for instance, the economy as a whole. At the present time, there are about one million divorces each year in the U.S. If the average party pays his or her attorney $20,000, that would generate a total of $40 billion per year. This covers only the fees of lawyers, and leaves out both the cost of the courts and the fees of marriage counselors. It seems not entirely unreasonable to suppose that the divorce industry grosses somewhere between one-half percent and one percent of GDP, but probably close to the one-half percent mark. I offer these figures as indicative only, and I do not vouch for their precise accuracy.

The Anthropology of Divorce

Among the social sciences, anthropology and economics bear a particularly intimate relationship because of the congruence of their subject matter. Economics deals with the way that individual choices aggregate to define the allocation of work and the assignment of scarce resources in society. Anthropology concerns itself with how the individual need for society defines societal roles and functions and builds shared expectations. Each science focuses its attention on a need—broadly defined—either the need for material goods or the need for social interaction and approval. It is not surprising therefore that it is in the end impossible to understand either one without having some appreciation for the other.

If the divorce society does not fulfill the demands of

individual persons for society, what kinds of social institutions will arise and how will they interact with the existing institutions of the broad community? The essential fact of the divorce society is that, other things being equal it is impossible for any person to make credible durable marriage vows. The law does not enforce them, and everyday experience brings ever more examples of their unreliability. This situation can be addressed by groups of citizens who form smaller, more cohesive groups which do not permit or do not recognize divorce. Divorce continues to occur, even among members of the group, but they are then excluded from that group. Subcultures of this sort, which provide various kinds of extraordinary supports for their members, arise all the time.

In America, we tend to identify them with ethnicity, because one of the most common needs for extra support came among immigrant groups, and these very conveniently sorted themselves out by place of origin. What is necessary is that the members perceive that the group helps them to deal with difficult circumstances, and that membership in the group is a privilege that can be revoked by the other members. There are many particular difficulties that a particular subculture could address. Very often in America they have encountered employment discrimination, for instance. All these particular motives are however subordinate to the more fundamental human need for society and social acceptance. The bedrock of culture is acceptance and approval.

Is it likely, or even plausible, that smaller societies of persons would form around the guarantee that within the group there is no divorce? I consider that to be not only plausible, but to be in fact nearly certain. From a purely financial point of view alone divorce is enormously costly. People therefore have a financial incentive—need, if you will permit—to change the expectations that arise from the divorce society and that sustain it as a social environment once established. One of the chief functions of a culture is to support shared expectations, and that is precisely the cure that is needed because the harm that comes from the divorce society lies in the expectations that it creates. A strong subculture can simply change those expectations for its members.

As the god Janus faces both forward and backward in time, so every subculture faces in two opposite directions: facing the persons who are its membership and facing the rest of society on their behalf. In regard to the members of a clique who have committed themselves to a rule of marriage without divorce, they will tailor their group in many ways to serve that end and to better suit their preferences, and about these nothing more can be said. But one need is certain to arise, and that is very strict excommunication of members who violate the code of conduct that defines the group. Any member who divorces must immediately be excluded, or else the group itself ceases to exist in any meaningful sense. This eventuality will arise from time to time, but in other respects the group can function quietly.

The relations between this group and the broader society are likely to be more controversial. Every distinct subculture exists in an environment of mixed tolerance and hostility from the surrounding culture, and these groups will be no different. Other groups within society, and society as a whole, naturally wish to engage the loyalty of all persons, and thus each particular group is to some extent a rejection of all the other groups, and may also be viewed as a rejection of society as a whole. Ethnic and religious minorities face this sort of suspicion all the time. Subcultures based on a single shared value—the

National Rifle Association comes readily to mind—also provoke hostility from outside. Even groups that are based on an activity, such as the Boy Scouts and the Girl Scouts, can find themselves at odds with other subcultures that feel threatened by them. The ongoing conflict between the homosexual community and the Boy Scouts is a case in point.

It is therefore a matter of some concern that groups that form around a commitment to marriage without divorce will find themselves in conflict with other groups that have opposing agendas and with a broad society that rebels at divisions within itself and seeks to form a single, seamless common culture. It is up to the law to mediate the inevitable conflicts fairly and justly, recognizing the citizens' right of free association. The example of the Boy Scouts is somewhat worrisome on that score, because the law appears at this juncture to be unwilling to defend that organization against the persecution by the gay community. There are other examples, the Amish being a notable one, who are left to themselves. As long as there are subcultures—and surely there will always be—adjudication conflicts between distinct groups and adjudicating conflicts between the demands of society as a whole and the member groups will be an essential function of the law, and also one of its most difficult ones.

Government in the Divorce Society

The effect of divorce, in the large, is to make women more dependent upon the welfare state. While men are able to provide for their material needs on their own, women who are mothers find that very difficult to do. One effect is the one I highlighted previously, which is that women from an early age devote more time and energy to investing in their own income potential and less investing in their husband's income potential. This greatly reduces the income loss that a wife and mother experiences at divorce. In most cases however, the husband was actually earning more than his own upkeep alone which left a surplus for the two to share, and that surplus is now gone. In other cases, the lack of investment in the husband's income potential will have wiped out the surplus and eaten into the necessities, but that of course does not leave either husband or wife better off or less dependent on public welfare. The fact remains that to the extent that the wife devotes herself to family and children, she is financially dependent. If she cannot depend on her husband, she has to depend on public welfare or public employment.

Several consequences follow from this dependency. First and most visible is the fact that the public, in whose name the administration governs, themselves become dependents on the government. Their decisions are necessarily skewed to serve their own self-interest: welfare programs proliferate and candidates for office promise better and bigger benefits. The proletariat class, consisting of persons whose livelihood depends on the state, grows. This is not disagreeable to the governors themselves, as long as the tax levies have broad public support, because it ensures that most elections will turn on issues that they understand and that to a large degree they command. In fact, so *un*-disagreeable is it that the government is very inclined to promote further dependency. One way to do so is to make divorce even simpler and easier to obtain than before.

This incentive completes the circle that I raised in talking about the law of divorce and the process by which the law is shaped. The law is crafted by a closed society of interested parties who need only satisfy each other and the administration and legislature completes that society. They appoint the judges and they enact the occasional revisions of the law. In this, they are on the one hand dependent on the legal clique of divorce attorneys and family courts judges, and on the other hand they have an unstated incentive to breed dependency on the welfare state.

In saying this, I do not deny that the legislature, in particular, can be motivated to enact legislation that shrinks the welfare state, if a sufficiently large and vocal public arises to demand it. Legislatures are a reflection of the public will when that will is expressed. The legislature would be willing—under sufficient duress—to make divorce harder to obtain. The problem that arises is that the faction that wants more divorces—the divorce industry—are always present and vigorous in defense of their interests, while a public that wants divorce made harder does not get paid to press its goals and has to take time out from other work to do it. It takes a tremendous surge of public indignation to offset the demands of any entrenched industry, and the divorce industry is in no way exceptional in this regard. This is especially true when the byproduct of easy divorce is welfare dependency among a large component of the public, because that also serves the interest of many legislators.

Conclusion

The theme that unifies and that energizes this essay is that divorce is not simply a personal decision, and is not even a decision confined to the family of parents and children. Divorce, like every other decision, has broader social ramifications because the actions of each person create the environment in which the rest of the public lives. This is an environment of daily realities, like the welfare dependency of divorced women, and just as importantly it is an environment of expectations. Other things being equal, when we see something being done commonly in society, we have to assume that each person that we deal with has a high propensity to do that too. This rational expectation becomes, moreover, self-sustaining or even becomes self-aggrandizing.

It would be easy for one to paint a lurid picture of ever-rising divorce rates; increasing welfare dependency; increasing corruption of the political process as the competition for shares of the welfare pie drowns out all other issues from the public forum; society divided into tight-knit groups built around the promise of marital fidelity; these groups viewed with suspicion and mistrust by the rest of society that, either from jealousy or alienation views them as subversive and potentially disloyal. In reality however, nothing is this easy. There are many forces that shape the formation of society, and divorce and its consequences are only one of them. Thus any such picture would be only a crude caricature of any actual society. It would have some justification nonetheless, as a model in which to bring the decline of the family and of commitment to the family into focus.

Marriage is actually a very simple institution. It is simply a small society in which a man and a woman help each other. While they are complete equals in this, the nature of the help they give is very different. Marriage is a partnership of very dissimilar equals, and indeed the only practical sense in which they can be viewed as equals is in their common shared humanity, and of course that they love each other equally. When they also have children to raise, this dissimilar equality becomes even more evident because the children are also in every sense equal to their parents even though their contribution to the family is tremendously different too.

Even in the face of a monumental divorce rate men and women continue to marry, and many of them do not divorce. That is both testimony to the importance of marriage to most persons, and testimony also to the capacity of individual men and women to swim against the current of the society around them. It is natural to take satisfaction in their independence and fidelity, but the fact that there are many such persons is not the answer to anything. Apologists for the *status quo* would naturally want to argue: "See, men and women still marry and stay married." Meaning, I suppose, that there is no problem here. This is a disingenuous line of reasoning, because it is tantamount to saying that the patient is doing fine up to the moment he stops breathing.

In any case, to reiterate, my agenda in putting together this essay is not to reform society. It is the more modest goal of promoting an understanding of the social ramifications of individual choices, and of the need always to take them into account.

Notes

1. I apply a 40 percent marginal tax rate to the $30,000 of income that the husband loses, which reduces his tax liability by $12,000. The wife still pays a 40 percent rate on her salary.

9

The Simple Algebra of Divorce

The Simple Algebra of the Divorce Rate

Since in the U.S. there are about two million marriages each year and one million divorces, it is fair to say that at the current rate half of all marriages will end in divorce. That rate certainly seems high enough to establish a very high expectation of divorce for each man and woman who is contemplating marriage, and who is planning his or her career. The rate of divorce in relation to marriages is not precisely the most meaningful statistics however. What we would really want to know is the proportion of persons who will divorce at some time in their lives. Since it is possible to divorce multiple times, this number must be somewhat smaller than one-half. It is possible to investigate that question, and I will address that topic here.

As we will see, the risk of divorce does not have to be the same for men and for women, but for the moment I will ignore this refinement, and will simply take "persons" to be the relevant class. Let us take the unknown X to be the probability that a person will ever marry and divorce. Similarly, let Y denote the number—as a percentage—of marriages that end in divorce. At the present time Y equal one-half, but there is no reason for now to pick any particular number. I will simply call it Y.

How many divorcees will there be in a given population, given that some of them will divorce more than once?

The fraction of all first marriages that end in divorce is equal to X, because there is no second marriage until the first is dissolved. Assuming that all divorcees remarry and that the risk of divorce is the same for first and second marriages, the $X*X$ is the number of second marriages that end in divorce. Similarly, under the same assumptions, $X*X*X$ is the number of third marriages that end in divorce. For simplicity, we can approximate the total number of divorces as

$$Y = X + X*X + X*X*X + X*X*X*X + \ldots$$

This is the familiar binomial series, which sums to

$$Y = X / (1 - X).$$

Now, we need to solve this equation for X, in terms of Y. Doing that gives us

$$X = Y / (1 + Y).$$

Now we can evaluate this expression for any value of Y, including $Y = 1/2$. At $Y = 1/2$, we find that $X = 1/3$. Under the assumptions that we made, about one-third of all persons would eventually divorce. One-ninth of all persons would divorce at least twice; one-twenty-seventh would divorce at least three times, and so on. To put these numbers in perspective, they imply that in a town of 29,000 persons, on average one thousand of them will divorce at least twice over the course of their lives, and about 330 of them will divorce three times or more.

This estimate is admittedly rough because it depends

upon some very simplistic assumptions. I have implicitly assumed that everyone marries, and that the only variable is the fraction of those marriages that end in divorce. I can get away with that assumption when it comes to counting the first divorces, because I can start not with the whole population, but with only that part who ever marry at all. By definition, all of them marry. But for counting subsequent divorces matters are not so simple. It makes a big difference what proportion of divorcees remarry. Let me denote by p_1 the probability that a person who has divorced once will remarry, and by p_2 the probability that a person who has divorced twice will marry for a third time, and so on. This defines a string of probabilities $p_1, p_2, p_3, \ldots$ Now the relationship between X and Y is more complicated, because the frequency of multiple divorces depends on the probabilities of remarriage. We have

$$Y = X + p_1 * X*X + p_1 * p_2 * X*X*X + \ldots$$

The factor p_1 appears in every term that follows because a person cannot divorce three times or more unless he or she marries at least twice. We can apply this formula to refine our estimate of the number of women who ever divorce. For women alone, I will use the letter W rather than X to denote the probability of divorce. We have

$$Y = W + p_1 * W*W + p_1 * p_2 * W*W*W + \ldots$$

Broadly speaking, women are unlikely to remarry. The factor called p_1 is for them rather small. For simplicity I will set it equal to zero. In other words, I will assume that divorced women never remarry. This is obviously an oversimplification, but it is close to the truth. In this case, all the terms after the first one are zero, so algebraically,

$$p_1 = 0,$$

$$Y = W + 0 * W*W + 0 * W*W*W + 0 \ldots,$$

$$Y = W = 1/2.$$

If half of all marriages end in divorce, and if women never remarry, then half of all women who marry will divorce.

This adjustment is roughly correct for women, but it is not true at all for men. Divorced men have a very high probability of remarriage. For men, the first few p factors are close to one. Obviously, no one remarries an infinite number of times. A simple but decent approximation is that men marry some fixed number of times, which I will call N times. So the first N of the p's are qual to one, and the others are all equal to zero. In reality, some men remarry once and some remarry many times. There is no single number N. For our purposes, the N that belongs in the formula is something like the average number of remarriages.

The other characteristic of men is the probability of subsequent divorce. I have up to now assumed that all marriages have the same probability of ending in divorce, no matter whether they were first marriages or one-hundredth marriages. In reality, subsequent marriages are more likely to end in divorce. For the sake of argument, I will assume—certainly a distortion of reality, but a useful benchmark case nonetheless—that all subsequent marriages end in divorce.

With these assumptions, and using M to denote the probability that a man will divorce, we can proceed as follows. M is equal to the number of men who ever divorce, and by assumption, each of these men actually divorces $N+1$ times. Thus

$$Y = M + M * 1 + M * 1 * 1 + \ldots, \text{ out to } N+1 \text{ terms.}$$

$$Y = M * (N + 1).$$

Now, to obtain an estimate for M we need to assign a value to N. Suppose that on average a man who divorces his first wife will marry twice more, so $N = 2$.

$$M = Y / (N+1) = .5 / (2+1) = 1/6.$$

As I stated previously, the frequency of divorce can be different for men and for women, and it is in fact much higher for women than for men. This is because a relatively few divorce-prone men leave behind a much larger number of divorced wives. To make this add up for the community as a whole, it must also be true that a much larger number of men never marry at all, since the total number of brides and grooms must be equal. If men had a sufficiently poor life expectancy, that could also bring the two into balance, because there would be fewer available grooms, but at the present time the unmarried men are not generally dying. They are simply remaining single.

To sum up, in the U.S. today the current divorce rate would leave a society in which on average one-third of all persons who marry eventually divorce. For women the proportion is much higher, and is actually close to one-half of all women. For men, the odds of divorce are smaller than one-third. Those men account for a disproportionate fraction of all the marriages and divorces, leaving a very appreciable pool of men who never marry at all.

What follows from this fact is that the expectations must also be quite different for men and for women. Women run a much greater risk of divorce than do men, and so have a greater incentive to change their expectations and the life plans to prepare for it.

More Algebra

In the course of discussing the algebra of divorce rates, I raised the equally important question of marriage rates. This is an interesting topic, and I will deal with it here in the same mathematical framework as the previous discussion.

The conclusion regarding the divorce rate is that close to one-half of women who marry will subsequently divorce. By similar reasoning, I came up with a figure that one sixth of all men who marry will divorce. These are by no means exact calculations. They are rough estimates at best, but in any case, I will simply use them in what follows without further question. They answer the question of what percentage of men and women who marry will eventually divorce, but they do not answer the equally interesting question of what percentage of all men and all women will experience divorce. The unknowns that we need to pin down are of course the marriage rates for men and women. I will use the letter p to denote the marriage rate of women and q to denote the marriage rate of men. It is popular knowledge that p is quite close to one, but I will not make any assumption about either p or q at this point.

Let MAR represent the percentage of all women who

marry, *MAR* is equal to the ratio of all marriages to the number of women. Since among adults of marriage age, the numbers of men and of women are almost exactly equal *MAR* is also equal to the ratio of marriages to the male population. Now, taking the women first, the number (i.e., percentage) of marriages is equal to p, by assumption.

$$MAR = p.$$

Since some men marry more than once, *MAR* is not equal to q. If q is the fraction of men who ever marry, how many marriages would they produce? We calculated before that one-sixth of men marry and divorce three times, and the other five-sixths marry once and stay married. Thus, five-sixths of the men cause one marriage and the other one-sixth cause three marriages. It follows that

$$MAR = 5\,q/6 + 3 * q/6 = 8\,q/6.$$

Now, since the frequency of marriages is the same for both (since the number of men and women is equal), we conclude that

$$p = 4\,q/3.$$

Equivalently,

$$q = .75\,p.$$

In words, the marriage rate of men is, under the assumptions I have made previously, 75 percent of the marriage rate of women. If, for instance, 90 percent of women marry, then about 68 percent of men marry at least once.

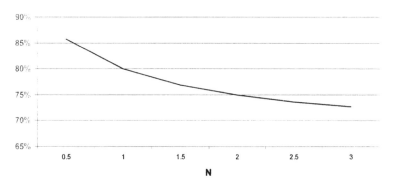

Men's Marriage Rate, as a Percent of Women's Rate

It would be helpful at this point to reconsider some key assumptions that went into this estimate, because it seems surprisingly low. The most problematical assumption was the factor called N, which is the number of times that divorced men will remarry and divorce again. I had used an estimate of $N = 2$. The following graph adds a kind of sensitivity analysis to this single point estimate. It shows values of N from .5 to 3, and shows the fraction that corresponds to each one. The figure on the vertical axis is the ratio of q / p. That is to say, it is the marriage rate of men as a fraction of the marriage rate of women.

The plausible range of marriage rates of men seems to extend between 73 percent and 85 percent. Since in today's world the numbers of young women and young men are about equal, the high divorce rate implies that a rather large percentage of men never marry.

The masculine marriage rate is a rather important statistic in its own right, but it leads to an even more interesting figure. We are now in a position to estimate what percentage of men who marry will eventually divorce: the *propensity* to divorce among men. We already have the corresponding estimate for women. It is 50 percent. I do not assume anything about causation of course. This is simply the percentage of married women who will divorce, for whatever reason. The corresponding propensity to divorce among men can be calculated as follows.

We know, given the assumptions we are working from, the one-sixth of married men who stay married nevertheless end up in divorce. That is the *conditional propensity to divorce.* What percentage of all men can expect to marry and to divorce? This is a particularly important number because it determines how young men, contemplating marriage for the first time, may view their prospects. There is at most a 75 percent chance that that he will marry, and given that he marries, a five in six chance that he will not divorce. Putting these together, about one in eight men will eventually divorce. This is a deliberate overestimate in one sense, because it assumes that all women marry.

This estimate brings into stark relief how different are the prospects of men and women. Assuming that all women marry, the average young women can estimate that she has about a fifty percent chance of experiencing divorce. The young man who sits next to her in study hall, by contrast, projects about one chance in eight of experiencing divorce. I do not need to reiterate that these numbers are all speculative and at best approximate, but the rough implication is hard to escape.

Notes

1. Strictly speaking, p_1 is the ratio of the probability of remarriage to the probability of an initial marriage.

Part Four

Sources of Law:
Natural Law, Common Law,
and Public Policy

10

The Command Trap: The Fallacy of Escalating Expectations

The federal government's job is big and it's massive, and we're going to do it. Where it's not working right, we're going to make it right. Where it is working right, we're going to duplicate it elsewhere.
—George W. Bush, speaking about the daunting job of rebuilding New Orleans

We are here to serve the public.
—Popular Misconception

I have elsewhere in this book identified political conservatism with one specific principle: the principle of limited government. That identification comes naturally within the context of American political thought, where it is rooted in the political ideas of Thomas Jefferson, and especially in the Declaration of Independence. His ideas are themselves an expression, or more properly a brilliant flowering, of a tradition of natural rights that goes back at least into the Middle Ages, and in that sense—in terms of their antiquity—they would easily be identified as "conservative." There are other connotations of the term "conservative," however, that seem to clash. Conservative seems to imply "prosaic," but the idea of limited government is a radical novelty in the context of human history. Conservative seems cautious or even timid, but the defense of natural rights has often demanded extraordinary courage and ruthless determination. Accordingly, there is more to "conservatism," to the idea of conservatism, than natural rights and limited government. There is another face, so to speak, of conservative political philosophy: one that seems instinctively more conservative. My goal in this essay is to put them together, side by side, to see what they have in common; to see what is truly conservative about each, and to see what they have to say about political organization.

The other side of conservatism is not timidity, nor is it cowardice, nor is it even the serenity of the old wisdom. The other fundamentally conservative idea of political philosophy is that society and its laws and customs grow organically, by a process that most closely resembles a complex natural ecosystem. The instinct to govern demands rules of law and demands formal lines of command and accountability. This tradition searches for customs rather than rules, and for loyalty rather than accountability. This is the tradition of English conservatism—although is clearest statement and defense were set out by the Irish Edmund Burke—whose proudest achievement is that England is governed wholly without a written constitution. The bedrock on which English law and rights are erected is not a written constitution, but an institution called the "common law."

The Common Law Tradition

The term "common law" refers to the body of judicial precedent which began in medieval England[1] and which continues today not only in England, but in several countries that had their roots as English colonies. The man most closely associated with the common law is not English, but American: Oliver Wendell Holmes, Jr. His treatise on the common law had, and continues to have, a profound influence on the development of jurisprudence throughout the English-speaking world. With the growing centralization of English government at London, the Parliament became increasingly active in writing legislation designed to impose the stamp of public policy and royal needs on judicial decisions, but by its nature the common law evolves naturally—"organically" so to speak—out of the accumulated decisions of judges whose mission is to resolve disputes that are brought before them. The idea of an autonomous legal system building on legal precedent rather than legislation was not new or unique to the common law. Across the Irish Sea to the west, Ireland had a similar but much older tradition known as "Brehon law."[2] Without doubt, moreover, this sort of law which accretes from judicial decisions is the norm in traditional societies.

Two attributes of the common law, and of any juridical tradition of law, stand out as clear and defining ideas. The first is that the law and the rights it recognizes emerge not from a central document, but arise from a rather Darwinian process of natural selection evolving from the gradual process of settling disputes between persons. This is the "conservative" law—the law which discovers essential rights by how they guide the well-meaning adjudication of cases one at a time. No single decision is of much weight, but each one adds its speck of sand to the whole edifice of the law. No ruling necessarily binds a court as it settles the case immediately at hand, but by the same token no decision is ever quite forgotten. As I noted above, the Brehon law of Erin predates even the written form of the Irish language, and its precedents were preserved in an oral tradition accreted over centuries. Common law judges are by profession judicial activists, because their highest calling is to render justice in the case at hand. Yet they are never legislators, because no subsequent court is bound strictly to mirror their rulings. The "law" is actually not the rulings as such, but the *obiter dicta*.

The other essential property, which is closely tied to the first one, is that the common law does not recognize any fixed edifice of "rights." Rights are a by-product of settling disputes among parties. As the nature and causes of disputes evolve, so also do the principles recognized by the law. Justice Holmes's gift to the common law was his enshrining this adaptability—this premise of judicial activism—at the center of the law. Without in any way diminishing Justice Holmes's contributions to our legal tradition, it is fair to underline at this point the fundamental difference with Thomas Jefferson and his inalienable rights. The two are not incompatible, and without doubt Justice Holmes revered Jefferson's Declaration as much as we do today, but they are different. It is in the nature of life moreover that wherever a difference is found, a conflict will eventually arise.

It may seem remarkable to us that it is possible—some would even say desirable—to have a system of laws and enforceable legal rights without necessarily relying on the sponsorship of any political authority, whether king or president or legislature. We take as granted that the rights of the people descend from the political authority, which defines them and which also manages public affairs. The preeminence of policy and of political authority has reached a pinnacle in modern times. For the most part that authority has been earned, as evidenced by the high standard of living and the high degree of personal safety achieved in modern society. At its worst, however, it has led to the notorious excesses of fascism and communism. These are degenerate political systems that both have their roots in "socialism," which is essentially a denial of inherent personal rights. Any nation that accepts the premise of socialism must necessarily look to its political authorities to create human rights, and of course to do so in ways that best serve the interests of the governor, rather than the interests of the governed.

The premise of socialism could be summed up in the following ideas. It is not the citizen who has rights. Any rights belong not to the person, but to the society at large. What the citizens have are wants and needs, which the society works to fulfill. However, the interests and desires of the individual are always subordinate to those of the society as a whole. There can be no fundamental conflict between man and society because the individual has no enforceable legal claim superior to whatever the society chooses to provide for him. The number of socialist polities has decreased sharply in recent years, but they do still exist.

Socialism is not merely a flawed system. It is an immoral system because it inverts the relationship between the people, who are moral agents, and the political establishment that supervises public affairs. That is to say, even in the modern age described by highly regulated societies we still view as corrupt those regimes that deny the natural right of man, and that choose instead to substitute the wishes of the governor for the superior rights of the people.

A Sidebar on Abortion "Rights"

The denial of human rights in favor of societal rights, while generally out of favor these days, has found fertile ground in the politics of "abortion rights." Even the most ardent supporter—or perhaps one should say *especially* the most ardent supporter—of elective abortion would concede that it is not a right as we use the term. It is a personal desire or perhaps a personal need which society chooses to accommodate. Abortion on demand is not promoted as a right, because it is predicated on a thesis that makes human rights irrelevant. Its natural extension is to justify mandatory abortion in the interests of the broader society, as it is practiced in China. The proposition that the people exist to provide new citizens for the nation, but only just the right number of new citizens, is a monstrous denial not only of particular human rights but of the very idea that human beings have any rights at all.

And on Liberalism

Liberalism has potentially a close affinity with conservatism but they are not the same. To emphasize the closeness with conservatism we would define liberalism as being devoted to the greatest possible freedom for the individual person. In practice, however, liberalism in recent times has often fallen under the spell of socialism. The reason for this is that liberalism does not define freedom, and so it is susceptible to the distorted concept of freedom that socialism promises. Since, if we accept the premise of socialism, the person has no inherent rights but has only those freedoms that the society grants, it seems that the person can have any freedoms that the law and society are inclined to create. Put more bluntly, the concept of right is discarded in favor of freedom, and the society—the state—is postulated as the source of those freedoms. Thus in practice "liberalism" consists of extracting from the society the maximum amount of freedoms: the maximum license.

This is a dead end, and it is the reason we draw a strict separation between liberalism and conservatism. Conservatism is premised on rights and liberalism on freedoms. Many freedoms—including many that are so often denied—are indeed rights. In parallel, many rights confer freedoms on the person, and indeed we say that the right of liberty is one of those inalienable rights granted to us by our Creator. But not all freedoms are ours by right because all rights bring with them the duties and obligations intrinsic in our moral nature. We are only as free to exercise our rights as we are free to fulfill our duties. These freedoms moreover do not come to us—as the socialists suppose—as gifts of a benevolent state. They come to us as inseparable from our human nature. Thus the state, as the conscious instrument of the society, exists to serve us, and not the other way around.

Edmund Burke on Conservatism and Society

The purpose of this seeming detour has been to bring us to Edmund Burke's starting point. His experience, in partnership with his moral instincts, led him to an organic, "conservative" idea of law and rights. His is the common law tradition. I have nonetheless insisted on separating Burke's vision of society from political conservatism, and the reason is that it endows the nation and its governors with excessive power and discretion. Since rights as Burke used the term are very particular—being precepts that bind a court of law as it weighs a particular cause of action—they are not directly tied to limitations on the government. They are not the same as the political rights of man that we accept as predetermining and restraining the rule of law.

Those well versed in the writings of Edmund Burke may find this judgment a bit peremptory. While he roundly denounced the French Revolution, and found particular cause for alarm that the revolutionaries had set out to write a constitution for their new republic, he was not willing to accept absolute monarchy. He fixed his political principles on the Glorious Revolution of 1689, in which King James II Stuart was driven from the throne and replaced by the dual monarchy of William of Orange and his wife, Mary Stuart. Edmund Burke's reasoning on this point is, however, obscure. What he seems to have liked about getting rid of the Stuarts and replacing them with William of Orange is that is was a minimal revolution. Every care was taken not to change anything except the monogram of the king. Thus the people—or more properly, the merchant class of London—were able to act out their distaste for the Stuart dynasty by this bloodless ritual without in any way undermining the stability of the state.[3] The Glorious Revolution did have a political objective, which was to break the alliance between England and France that had prevailed since the ascension of Henry VII Tudor to the English throne, so it would not be accurate to say that it was a complete irrelevance historically, but nothing in the laws and form of government was changed.

True to his gradualist inclination, Burke was not opposed to change entirely. He approved change that happens gradually and by means of a process or microscopic adjustments to the society and the nation. Conservatives certainly agree that gradualism is by no means an evil or something to be avoided. The disastrous course that the French Revolution took is evidence enough of the wisdom of Burke's criticism. It is also true that Burke defended the American Revolution, on the grounds that Britain was merely trying to enslave her colonies in order to enrich herself, and in violation of accepted rights of English citizens. But gradualism is not conservatism, because it consciously avoids making demands on the direction in which the evolution will take. That is to say, it simply ducks the issue of fundamental human rights. Conservatism demands a vision of right and wrong which in turn defines prior and inalienable human rights. Gradualism—while in many ways admirably "conservative"—leaves the state as the arbiter of rights. The rights which London was denying to English colonists were not, in his view, inalienable rights. They were simply those rights that Parliament had up to that point in time chosen to guarantee to subjects of the English crown.

The creed of conservatism was written not by a common law judge, but by Thomas Jefferson, the revolutionary. It draws its inspiration, moreover, not from caution and gradualism, but from an absolute. Not from common law, but from natural law.

The legal tradition of natural law, so admirably and succinctly expressed by Jefferson, is as old as the common law, though it flourished in the Latin countries of Western Europe. It was St. Thomas Aquinas who have it voice: *Lex Malum, Nullum Est.*[4] A law that promotes evil is null and void. The citizens are not bound to follow and may indeed be bound to defy such a law, because the government is not above the moral law.

The Law as Public Policy

With the spread of regulated society, which in the last half century has remarkably become the normal state of affairs in the world, the tie between law and government has been elevated to an exceptional degree. In part this trend is the result of the spread of representative government which very self-consciously predicates its authority on the will of "the people." Even modern tyrannies, both fascist and communist, have however been largely accorded the same kind of legitimacy as the true democracies are. As a result—and I emphasize that while the flowering of this trend is recent, the roots extend back over the millennia—rule-making by branches of the government has become widely accepted. There are two broad kinds of policy laws: those that interpose themselves into the judicial process to dictate rulings and those that create new agencies which have been accorded the power to make specific kinds of new law on their own authority. This novel aspect of law—as a body of rules fixed by the political authority—represents a challenge both to the common law tradition and to conservative principles of limited government. More importantly, it represents a potentially dangerous intrusion of discretionary authority—the sovereign authority of the government—into the legal relationships among the citizens and between them and the other important institutions of society.

On Actionable Rights Created by Legislation

Some legislative acts are simply intended to tie the hands of judges and to dictate how they proceed to settle disputes between contending parties. They supplant previous precedent by creating actionable rights directly. There are innumerable examples of this in American law. One of the more familiar areas in employment law, in which the rights of employees—and to a much lesser degree, employers—are imposed by legislation. Judges, despite our common law tradition, have little if any discretion is settling disputes that involve the rights and duties spelled out by this legislation. One must bear always in mind that "little" is not the same as "none," and the creativity of judges should not be ignored, but the intent of the Congress and the States is to restrain it tightly. This limitation is reflected in the fact that the Congress not only defined rights and procedures for resolving employment disputes, but created a parallel court system of administrative law courts to enforce it, thus bypassing the existing common law courts.

It is natural and inevitable that the legislature act infrequently, and that those occasional rulings should then undergo a lengthy process of testing and winnowing as they become incorporated into the body of common law precedent. When the legislature represents the people directly, the authority to establish actionable rights falls well within the limitations that define limited government. Far from presenting a bar to legislative activism, the popular mandate is an express authorization for the legislature to participate directly in legal process by which disputes are settled and rights clarified. Perhaps the law is too important to be left to the judges alone; the public definitely thinks so.

In practice, legislation is a very slow and clumsy tool for fashioning the law. First of all, there is the problem of limited accountability. Only very rarely does a legislature face an issue so broad and energized that the members must fear the popular wrath. Matters of that importance do arise from time to time. In terms of the American Congress, the civil rights laws of the 1960s and the laws regarding the rights of organized labor in the 1930s and 40s had that kind of impact. At the present time [2005 A.D.] laws regarding the rights of the family may rise to that level. Even when an issue clearly becomes a popular cause, however, with vociferous demonstrations of the popular will, the Congress is remarkably free and willing to avoid making any decision. I do not know personally of any member of Congress who has lost a seat because the Congress has been unable to address abortion on demand. I could not say that no one has paid at the polls for that silence, but if there has been anyone, he has gone quietly into retirement. The laws in these matters have been left entirely to the judicial process. Those who seem to be outraged by judicial activism do not seem somehow to be equally agitated by legislative ineptitude. This complaint, moreover, could be leveled equally by people on both sides of the matter.

The resistance of legislatures to tackle hard issues stems not only from a lack of accountability, but stems also from the nature of legislation itself. Any piece of legislation can at best assert a few general principles, but the disputes that raise before the law are very specific. The judicial process is designed to resolve particular issues one at a time, and judges and attorneys are only too aware of the grey areas that lurk on the frontiers of legal principles. A legislative approach necessarily lacks the flexibility that the courts take for granted.

The criminal law is perhaps the most pressing areas where this mismatch arises: the mismatch between general principles and context-driven judgement. The public naturally assumes that crimes are defined by law, but that is a misconception. In an earlier chapter I explained that the definition of a particular crime—the definition of what a specific defendant is charged with—incorporates many surrounding details which shape its social impact. Thus, as one example that is sometimes particularly relevant, crimes committed by persons who are abusing a position of trust—e.g., crimes by public authorities—are by their nature more serious than the same crimes between strangers. The reason is that a betrayal of trust compounds the particular harm of the crime, attacking simultaneously the particular victim and the basis for trust in legitimate authority. No feasible criminal code could substitute for the judicial process in which all the relevant aspects of the crime are brought to light and judged.

To summarize, legislative intervention into the juridical process and into the common law, in the case of American law, is by its nature limited, and it is not in principle a violation of limited government. Quite the contrary, law by public policy is much rarer than it should be, rather than being too common or intrusive. It is only under the most pressing circumstances that legislators are motivated to act, and it is only under similarly exceptional circumstances that they are required to risk any serious public censure for either inaction or mal-action.

It is always, moreover, within the power of the judges to eviscerate legislation that they find objectionable. The recent Kelo decision by the Supreme Court is a rather stunning illustration of the capacity of the courts to dispense even with guarantees of rights that are enshrined in our Constitution. The Fifth and Fourteenth amendments to the Constitution were, one would assume, added to guarantee rights of private property and of property-like rights (e.g., patents and copyrights) against acts of government. But as these amendments read, such rights are made conditional on something called "due process of law," without defining what that means. Over the last seventy years the Supreme Court has progressively gutted this phrase of any substantive meaning. "Due process" is now understood to mean whatever the public authorities say it means, on a case-by-case basis. I will return in a subsequent chapter to the matter of the Constitution, so I will not dwell on this topic here, except to point out what it implies about the comparative efficiency of the legislature and its declarations—even ones that have undergone the much more grueling test of adoption as an amendment to the Constitution—as compared with the common law and the judicial process.

On Legislation Creating Regulatory Agencies and the Fallacy of Command

The preceding section dealt with one area of tension between legislature and courts: between law as public policy and law as conflict resolution. In the matter of defining actionable legal rights, there does not appear to be any fundamental or systemic conflict, nor is there any natural tendency to infringe upon the principle of limited government. That does not of course rule out mistakes—especially ones made by an overly intrusive legislature—but in every aspect of life we are accustomed to deal with and rectify mistake. Beginning about a century ago a new dimension of public policy began to emerge. Starting from modest beginnings, it expanded to an encompassing vision of public agencies wielding the authority of the Congress to direct and manage many specific areas of national life. The astonishing transformation of economic organization and of scientific and technological knowledge seemed to demand it, because some sort of management, some sort of ruling powers, seemed to be called for to deal with matters that had never arisen before, and on which the common law was therefore silent.

This development was of course not limited to the U.S., and the terms "Congress" and "common law" could be adapted to the legal structures of nearly every nation. Regulatory agencies are essentially universal. What all have in common is that agencies of the government are created and endowed with great governing powers—powers to discern, legislate, and enforce judgements of public policy—that seemingly never existed before. In the American implementation, some of the new offices and powers have been added to the existing administration that reports to the president, but to a remarkable extent they have given rise to new agencies that exist outside the three constitutional branches of government. On paper, and perhaps in reality, this has been done so as to preserve for the Congress fairly strict control over how these powers are used and to sideline the executive branch of government. The effect has been to leave these various agencies, commission, authorities, and administrations with a very high degree of independent action and very weak political oversight. On the rare occasions when the same party holds both the White House and a majority in the Congress, the executive branch has presumably more leverage to manage them, but they were designed to be autonomous and that seems to be the reality.

There is, of course, great potential for these new powers subordinated to public policy to abuse the legitimate rights and freedoms of society, including the rights of individuals and the rights of other social institutions. Elsewhere in the world, this passion to regulate everything, in the name of some undefined common good, has unleashed the worst totalitarian instincts of government. We as individual citizens are quick to recognize intrusions on our personal liberties, and one could easily find cases where they have been violated, but for the most part the right that is most often impaired is the right of free persons to combine into various organizations and private associations for their mutual benefit. By far the most numerous of such institutions are businesses but there are many others: churches, labor unions, schools, fraternal and neighborhood associations, professional societies, and probably other similar organizations that I am overlooking.[5] These are also citizens of the nation by construction. The right of free association guarantees to the people the right to form them and to adapt and use them as long as they—the institutions—are good citizens, respecting the rights of others and avoiding criminal behavior. In particular, the right of free association bestows on the members the authority to govern their own institutions as they see fit.

The greatest failure of liberalism—of liberal political doctrine—has been to routinely dismiss all these institutions in favor of a single focus on the individual citizen. The right of free association is one of the most important and valuable of all those inalienable rights that our Creator has bestowed on us. It is quite true that only actual persons are moral agents, having intrinsic moral worth, and that all these other associations are in some sense fictions. They are nonetheless genuine citizens because without them the people would be unable to use and defend their personal human rights; unable to make them effective. Persons shorn of the right of free association have for all intents and purposes no other rights either; and any government which under color of public policy attacks the right of free association is preparing its human citizens for serfdom. Limited government therefore implies government that respects the rights not only of the public, but also the rights of the other institutions that they have created to serve them. The rights—the civil or citizenship rights—of private institutions comprehend the liberty to be governed by the legitimate wishes of the members. The government has no more right, acting in the name of public policy, to demand servile labor from them than it is entitled to demand servile labor from the people. The government has no right to intrude on the governance of private institutions and organziations than it has the right to intrude on the freedoms of the people.

These are important general principles, though they seem to be often violated in practice. Agencies that have been created by the government and that answer to it are very liable to abuse their powers, as these principles suggest, and the way they are constituted makes abuse more likely and more dangerous. It is what I have called the "command fallacy."

Quite simply put, the command fallacy is a trap that beckons anyone who has been given power to impose his wishes on the public, on the basis of his presumed superior wisdom and knowledge. Suppose that the Congress has created a regulatory board with a mission to oversee some aspect of commerce. It could be the Federal Reserve Board—an example that I will return to in a moment—or the Securities Exchange Commission or the Food and Drug Adminstration. The directors of the board are chosen for their proven expertise and endowed with the authority to govern, which means to impose their will on, the various persons and institutions that deal in that business.

This hypothetical board was created because the Congress was unhappy with how those citizens were making out on their own. It seemed that they need more direction, and that may be true. So the board is in command, and has the power to issue specific laws by decree. How does that responsibility look from the perspective of the decision makers on the board? They can simply sit back, collect their handsome salaries, give pompous speeches in Switzerland, and let the world follow its own inclinations. George Stigler and others have made a compelling case that that is precisely the course of action that a rational board member will follow.[6] Stigler asks why would someone who, as the saying goes, already has it made set out to antagonize the one class of parties—the regulated—who has the capacity to make him look bad? This line of reasoning and empirical research goes under the name of the "capture theory" of economic regulation, on the premise that the regulator is eventually captured by the major regulated institutions.

Captured boards of regulators have the capacity to do much harm, and what I have termed the "command fallacy" also applies to their tendency to make bad policy, but the command fallacy is more easily explained in the context of a regulatory board that has maintained its independence and its commitment to its original mission. I will assume therefore that the board is completely faithful to its mission and is not infected with cronyism. The mission they have been entrusted with is to change the way that the regulated parties interact with each other and with the rest of society. There was something about the way they were dealing in the past that the Congress was deeply unhappy with and wanted to change. Toward that end, the Congress not only created the new board, but filled it with recognized experts. Now, the board—whose mission I need not specify because these remarks apply in general—knows from the start that if they do nothing, or if they have no effect, they are failing to accomplish the purpose for which they were designated, and they know that the "effect" is measured by how much a difference they can bring about amongst the regulated. A third fact quickly asserts itself. The effectiveness of the board can be measured by how unhappy are the regulated and how vociferously they object and criticize. An important aspect of the board's mission is to consciously ignore the opinions of the parties—persons and institutions—that they regulate, and it was to be able to do so that they were given their authority directly from the Congress.

This leaves a rather embarrassing question behind, which is how does the board know when they are doing a good job? How do they know when they are actually improving the functions of the regulated? The board exists to define and to impose laws of public policy on parts of society because the objects of their policies would otherwise harm themselves or the public. This charter by its nature tends to disqualify the wishes of the regulated. It is for this reason that the board is staffed with persons who are recognized experts in the particular topic of regulation, and we assume that their expertise is genuine and valuable. The command fallacy is not in itself a cause of bad policies and bad jdugements. It is however a trap that tends to perpetuate bad decisions and bad judgements. Once the board launches on a mistaken policy, the almost certain immediate result is that the regulated will start to complain. But the board must then confront a fundamental issue, which is whether these particular protests are the result of bad decisions by the board, or are they the result of good decisions. Good decisions are very likely to be just as unpopular as bad ones. As a result the feedback from the regulated is necessarily discounted.

I emphasize again that I am not arguing that regulators prefer bad judgments or that the constitution of regulatory bodies somehow biases them in that direction. On the contrary, I accept that most of the decisions are good. But the mission of the regulator is itself a trap that cuts it off from some of the most important feedback that it needs. The worse the decision, moreover, the more resistant—the blinder—the regulator is to the natural signs that a mistake has been made. The grant of rule-making or law-making power makes it possible for my hypothetical board to bull straight ahead in the face of widespread opposition. Other powerful bodies, including of course the Congress itself, are naturally disinclined to intervene. They created the board to legislate and implement public policies of a highly technical nature where the Congress itself possesses no expertise, and they are sure to be very unwilling to—or even deeply hostile to—the idea of second-guessing the experts.

Of all the public bodies empowered to Congress to make policy and to put it into action, the most respected and the most influential is without doubt the Federal Reserve Board. Its history therefore provides a rich harvest of examples in which the board followed a mistaken policy relentlessly to the grave. Although it is no longer headline news, the record of bad judgement by the Federal Reserve Board that led to the crash in 1929 and the subsequent Great Depression is highly instructive both because of the magnitude of the mistakes and the thoroughness with which they have been documented and blame assessed. The standard account of monetary policy in the depression was written by Milton Friedman and published in his work on American monetary history.[7]

Milton Friedman is known for his commitment to *Laissez-faire* markets, and for his deep mistrust of regulatory offices imposed on them by political powers. Over the years his trenchant criticism of monetary policy of the Federal Reserve Board has become a cornerstone of conservative thought. He has been noted throughout his career as a critic of activist eonomic policy, arguing that it has consistently worked more harm than good. His studies in macroeconomics, for which he was honored with a Nobel prize, lend no support to the view that has been promoted under the name of "Keynesianism," that the modern market economy is inherently unstable and that it needs a lot of top-down supervision to avoid derailing. Quite the contrary, the private agents in the economy and the decision of the public are consistently, though not invariably, stabilizing while the imposition of public policy rules and initiatives—from the Fed, the Congress, or other actors—has been consistently a source of instability.

The problem with active economic management is that the experts who are expected to direct it are frequently wrong because they feel the need to make bold decisions—the ones that they were given their powers to make—before the nature of the apparent crisis and its causes are known. Thus to the degree that they are expected to respond to current events with "solutions," they are being required to guess, to gamble. While there is no complete account of why the economic and business affairs of a nation proceed unevenly as a sequence of "expansions" and "contractions," a great deal is known. It apears that as time passes, the economy is buffeted by shocks, coming in a range of sizes and impacting randomly all the corners of the complex web of ecnomic relations.[8] As I write, hurricane Katrina has wreaked its destruction on the Gulf coast. Exactly how that shock will spread to the oil and natural gas businesses, and to other sorts of businesses that function on the Gulf coast remains a speculative mystery. This is only one example of the kind of shock leaders of business and government expect the Federal Reserve Board to address with steps that will minimize the damage done, but there is no consensus what that would be. The Board can create money and make it available to people and to institutions that have found themselves temporarily strapped for cash because of the hurricane damage, but doing so inevitably cheapens the dollar. If the damage from the hurricane—the damage to the national economy—is large, a large expansion of the money supply would be warranted even if it will result in a lot of inflation. On the other hand, any depreciation of the dollar will itself be another shock that disrupts economic relationships. So, how much money to create? How much good will the right answer accomplish? How much disruption will the wrong answer spread? In hindsight we may know, but hindsight is not management or policy. Even then it is unlikely that in hindsight we will know, because other shocks of all kinds will have added more confusion.

The story of the monetary policy that caused the Great Depression is the story of a board pursuing policy goals that were at best tangential to its mission. The proper goal of the Federral Reserve Board, in the view of Milton Friedman, was to make monetary policy as nearly netural as possible, in the sense of taking the necessary steps to prevent shocks in the money stock of the economy from distorting economic relationships—the prices of valuable assets—and from sending misleading signals about prices and wages. That is not an easy job, because it requires that the board assess the nature of current events and discern which ones are distorting pricing signals by separating real from nominal prices, and which reflect real changes in economic relationships. The mission of the Fed is to take steps to offset the former without causing or contributing to the latter. It is not their mission to manage reality. Yet they are repeatedly implored to use the power of a central bank—the power to print money that costs nothing and to spend it to purchase things that have real value—to correct real shocks.

In the Great Depression the fundamental policy mistake of the Fed was to tie its actions to European politics and political crises. The Bank of England had tried, following the disastrous lead of Sir Winston Churchill, to defend the value of the pound sterling. The pound was under intense pressure as a result of the general strike of 1928, and it was thought that a vigorous defense—which means in practice a very contractionary monetary policy—was needed to reassure nervous capitalists.[9] The Federal Reserve agreed to a parallel policy, in the interest of stabilizing the dollar / pound exchange rate. That was in a sense a very forgivable mistake; stabilizing exchange rates is a good thing other things being equal. But once they fixed on that as the preeminent goal, they were unable to revisit that decision. The growing distress that tight money was causing around the country was deemed to be not a reason to change goals, but a gratifying sign that they were successfully accomplishing the one they had intended to do. The experience of the Great Depression shows not only that the board is very capable of mistaking its mission, but is then highly resistant to doubting itself.

Over the last twenty years, under the guidance of Chairman Alan Greenspan, the Federal Reserve has adopted the goal of defending the value of the dollar, although it has been able to manage around this goal when business conditions warranted. As a result, the dollar has been stable, and has unquestionably justified its stature as the world reserve currency. Over the last eight years or so, however, evidence has accumulated that the dollar is in fact *too* valuable, and that the Federal Reserve has in a sense been too successful. Monetary policy is no longer simply a matter of supplying money to the banking system. It is increasingly necessary to direct policies toward the whole finance industry, because the walls that separated bank money from other financial assets are no longer controlling. It is at the same time increasingly necessary to coordinate Fed policy with the policies of foreign governments and to respect their goals. In part because of these interdependencies and in part because of the convictions of the members of the board, there has been a refusal to rethink monetary policy in light of the warning signs that it has become harmful. When the existing policies are actually acheiving the intended purposes, who on the board is going to question whether they are good policies? They are "working." Command sets a trap for itself.

The success of monetary policy in recent years has greately expanded the power of the Federal Reserve, and insulated it further from criticism or opposition. It has also, and more importantly, made the Fed larger and more powerful than the private market institution that it was created to tame. In 1920, the Fed was a valiant neophyte sent off to tame a mystifying wilderness. By 2000, it was a dominating presence tending a thoroughly tame formal Versailles garden. Whereas there was previously an obstinate "reality" to confront, there is now only a slavish, captive financial industry to feed. In the short run, the Fed will always achieve its goals because there is no vocal opposition. For this reason, at the present time it does not get any useful feedback from the markets that answer to it. Thus it is that the more commanding is the commander, the deeper is the trap.[10]

Up to this point in the discussion I have not reeally brought in the implications of the presient and his subordinates. Many of the specialized agencies are already subordinated directly to the White House. Housing them within the executive branch is tantamount to subordinating them to a higher court of appeal. They can be forced to justify their decisions to the White House, just as judges can be forced to account to a higher court for their decisions. That is a very interesting aspect of the structure of policy making in the government and certainly deserves much further thought, but it does not actually change the dynamic of the command fallacy.

Limited Government and Law as Public Policy

The example of the common law should provide a healthy antidote to the more dangerous extremes of public policy. The common law has thrived because it avoids big decisions and broad policies in favor of tinkering. At the same time, because it grows progressively by the force of precedent, it is a kind of ongoing Darwinian ecosystem, discovering durable general principles and fundamental rights by a survivial principle. It is quintessentially "conservative," with a small c.

When the rule of law is viewed as a public policy, by contrast, it is inherently unlimited. The command fallacy guarantees that policy makers come to see their mission as that of defying and overcoming limits. They quite understandably do not suppose that the Congress and the president invested them with the powers to regulate and to govern just so they would have to surrender to limits. Far from it; everything in their charter says that they have been commissioned to defeat them. Inevitably it begins to seem that the work of the governors is too big and too important to let the rights of the governed get in its way.

The natural limitations of a government are the compass of what it does well. As I have explained above, this is not a call for small government or minimal government. There are occasions in which governments need to be large and imposing. Smallness is not a virtue in itself. Far less is it an endorsement of anarchy. It is rather a call to realism, and to realistic humility on the part of those who govern. "What is it that the public needs to have done and that you do well?" It is not enough to say that there is something that the other organs of society cannot do for themselves. There are many things that we are not able to do, including our inability to sprout wings and fly. The charter of the government is not co-extensive with those nice things that we are not able to do. It is constrained to those things that we cannot do otherwise and that the government does well.

On the first page of this chapter, I quoted President Bush on his promise to rebuild New Orleans. Why does Mr. Bush want to "rebuild" New Orleans and why does he think he would be good at it? Did he or some predecessor in the White House build New Orleans? Did he build New York or Washington or Helsinki for that matter? When did anyone ever say that building cities is a public function that has been relegated to the federal government? Most people were under the impression that cities come into being when lots of private citizens follow the lure of a better life to add their talents and to commit their fortunes to a burgeoning settlement. We always thought that it was people who built cities by moving there, and that it was for them to decide where it would be best for them to live and work. It is entirely understandable that the existing political structure of New Orleans and environs want the city rebuilt, because their importance is a direct function of the size and wealth of the city. It is also entirely understandable that the existing political organizaton finds a very sympathetic ear in Washington. What is however less than clear is why any of this is a good idea for the rest of us. Some contrary voices have weighed in with what appears to be a deep hostility to New Orleans. They seem to prefer that New Orleans disappear from the face of the earth. That is equally irresponsible. If people want to move to New Orleans and build a great new city, how can anyone else complain? No one of us has the slightest idea whether there should be a city where New Orleans stands, but we should be able to agree that it is not a question of public policies and of public commitment. Cities exist where—in Lenin's words—the people have voted with their feet to place them.

Because of the command fallacy, however, public policy and the process of formulating new policies are not naturally self-limiting. Quite the opposite; they are naturally self-aggrandizing.

Governments are accorded a wide latitude in the way they manage public affairs, because there is a constant need for good policy decisions. We do not live in that sort of static society where nothing new ever arises and where it is sufficient to apply and reapply tested principles. The world changes and governors are given the authority to take the lead in addressing new demands and new crises. It is nonetheless a great mistake to think that every new challenge needs a novel solution. Precedent, the messy baggage of past judgments, needs to be respected. The accumulated body of precedent needs to be developed. In addition, express judicial oversight—common law oversight—of policy decision is needed. Otherwise, the rights and freedoms of the public and of the many other private institutions of society are always at risk. The citizens have a right to the power to force their governors and regulators to publicly justify their chosen policies, and to make them clear hurdles not only of desirarbility but of feasibility. The reality of limited government means, to repeat, that the governors and their designees only have the power to impose goals and policies that are both desirable and feasible. Limited government is one that undertakes only what is worthwhile, and among the many worthwhile purposes, those that the government will be able to accomplish but that the public could not. Even within a general program, the limited government should shoulder only those parts that also meet these two tests.

Notes

1. The term "common law" signifies that it was intended to be the national law of England, held "in common" throughout the realm.
2. Brehon law actually predates not only any established Irish legislature, it predates the written form of the Irish language. It was preserved as largely oral tradition until the fifty century, when it was codified by Saint Patrick and his assistants. The word *Brehon* means "lawyer," and unlike the common law judges, who were appointees of the king of England, there were no permanent judges.
3. This remarkable neatness was actually an illusion, as Edmund Burke had to be well aware. The rebellion that was bloodless in England triggered a horrendous bloodletting in Erin, where James attempted to make his stand. It provoked moreover a determination on the part of the English government to find a final

solution to the Irish problem. The nature of this solution is clear from a short essay written a few years later (1729) by Dean Jonathan Swift in which he proposed—ironically, for he was a friend of the Irish—that the Irish people should be encouraged to eat their children in order to survive the misery and starvaton that had become their lot: see "A Modest Proposal for Preventing the Children of Poor People in Ireland from Being a Burden to their Parents or Country, and for Making them Beneficial to the Public." This widely read work did much to advance Swift's reputation as both a prose artist and a bleeding heart, but cooler heads did not let it distract them from the goal of exterminating the Irish people.

4. Thomas was by no means a radical by nature. He was by birth a crown prince of the kingdom of Naples. He however had experience early on in opposing higher authority. As a young professor at the University of Paris his writings came to the attention of the reactionary Cardinal Archbishop of Paris. The archbishop publicly banned his works from being distributed in the city. Thomas, not intimidated, appealed to the pope, who overruled the archbishop. Thomas went on to become the most respected of all Catholic philosophers, called affectionately the "sacred doctor."

5. More significantly, this list omits the single most important institution of all, which is marriage and family. This one form of association is of such vital importance that it deserves separate treatment.

6. George Stigler's writings on the logic and effects of regulation of economic activity are too extensive to sumarize in a footnote. The first, seminal paper, however, reveals a great deal about his thinking. In his article "What Can Regulators Regulate? The Case of Electricity," *Journal of Law and Economics* (1962) he dismissed the mythology of regulatory good intentions and turned instead to the question of whether in fact regulation makes any difference. Not surprisingly, he found no evidence of any effect of regulation (at the state level) of electric utilities. There are many other economists who have delved into this topic, including a second man whose research earned Nobel laurels: James Buchanan.

7. Milton Friedman and Anna J. Schwartz, *Monetary History of the United States, 1967 to 1960* (Princeton, N.J: Princeton U. Press, 1963). Princeton University Press; Princeton, NJ: 1963) I would recommend also a later book by Milton Friedman: *The Optimum Quantity of Money and Other Essays,* Chicago, IL: University of Chicago Press, 1969). University of Chicago Press: Chicago, Ill.

8. This story of the business cycle, as the byproduct of all kinds of

large and small random shocks, was pioneered by the great Soviet economist, Eugen (Yevgeny) Slutsky.

9. Marxist theory had so penetrated the mentality of Europe that very little was needed to convince business that the next Bolshevik revolution was at their doorstep. England was by no means unique in that respect. Conditions were far more dire in Germany, impoverished by the Treaty of Versailles, and revolution more threatening, but no nation was immune.

10. See my essays "Perfectly Inefficient Markets," and "Market Inefficiency as an Absorbing State," which are available on our web site: www.logisticresearch.com.

11

The Constitution and Natural Rights

It is taken as a truism by most people that the Constitution of the United States is the cornerstone of American law. At the present time the Congress is weighing Judge John Roberts for elevation to the Supreme Court, and as he makes his case before the Senate Judiciary Committee, the common theme of nearly all the questions is whether in his view this or that right is guaranteed in the Constitution. He has by all accounts charmed the senators while ducking most of those questions, by responding as a common law judge should: a common law judge draws upon the vast body of common law precedent to guide him in resolving particular disputes. It is quite impossible for him to form any opinion about how he would rule in hypothetical cases that are created to raise philosophical issues. A judge resolves actual disputes that are brought to him by real people, arising out of real factual situations.

Each age is characterized by its own distinctive issues. Today the sound and fury are launched on the matter of elective abortion and the Supreme Court decision in the matter of Roe vs. Wade. Inevitably, many of the questions to Judge Roberts had to do with that decision. As we consider the correlation between the Constitution and natural rights, I too will have occasion to comment on abortion and Roe vs. Wade.

The Constitution

One important truth that is too often overlooked is that the Constitution is not, and was never intended to be, the legal basis for human rights and freedoms. The Bill of Rights addresses questions of human rights directly, but it is not, and does not claim to be either the source of rights or even a complete catalog of them. I have explained in a previous chapter the importance of the natural law basis for human rights and freedoms. Thomas Jefferson, in the Declaration of Independence, got right to the point:

We hold these truths to be self-evident, that all men are created equal, that they are endowed by their Creator with certain unalienable Rights, that among these are Life, Liberty and the pursuit of Happiness—That to secure these rights, Governments are instituted among Men, deriving their just powers from the consent of the governed.—That whenever any Form of Government becomes destructive to these Ends, it is the Right of the People to alter or to abolish it, and to institute new Government, laying its Foundation on such principles and organizing its Powers in such Form, as to them shall seem most likely to effect their Safety and Happiness. Prudence, indeed, will dictate that Governments long established should not be changed for light and transient Causes; and accordingly all experience hath shewn, that Mankind are more disposed to suffer, while Evils are sufferable, than to right themselves by abolishing the Forms to which they are accustomed. But when a long Train of abuses and usurpations, pursuing invariably the same Object, evinces a Design to reduce them under absolute Despotism, it is their Right, it is their Duty, to throw off such Government, and to provide new Guards for their future Security.

The government that men and women have empowered to manage the affairs of the community and the nation is not the source of rights and freedoms. Fundamental rights are embedded in the constitutions of human beings, by grant of their Creator. The government does not confer rights; it serves them. It follows that fundamental human rights are not derived from the Constitution of the government. A constitution defines the organization of the government and defines its legitimacy.

This proposition may seem disturbing and even shocking in the context of the adulation of the Constitution today, under which it is almost universally assumed that the Constitution is both the full statement of the rights of the citizens, and actually the source of those rights. The Declaration of Independence clearly contradicts these errors, but the Bill of Rights of the Constitution also does. Article Nine of the Bill of Rights reads as follows:

Amendment IX:
The enumeration in the Constitution, of certain rights, shall not be construed to disparage others retained by the people.

This clause contemplates that there are other rights belonging to the people that are not stated or implied in the text of the Constitution or its amendments. If, moreover, the Constitution is not a complete enumeration of human rights, then quite obviously it cannot be the source of rights. Because of the Roe decision, the right of privacy has become a contentious issue, and one point of contention has been whether there is such a right "in the Constitution." Article Nine states expressly that it does not matter whether the right of privacy is asserted in the Constitution. If courts recognize it by common law precedent as a fundamental human right, then that is a settled matter. It is simply one of those human rights that are not explicitly addressed in the Bill of Rights. In point of fact, however, as Judge Roberts explained in testimony before the Senate, the right of privacy is clearly asserted by reference in the Bill of Rights. The prohibition of unreasonable search and seizure is part of the larger right of privacy, and could actually be interpreted to be the complete right of privacy. In any case, however, it is not necessary that the right of privacy be promised in the Constitution for it to be a guaranteed right of the citizens. We will see that the right to privacy is one of the most fundamental of all human rights, and is an indispensable companion of limited government.

The Constitution is a general law, adopted by a national legislature and confirmed by the people directly or, in the case of American practice, by the states. This extra affirmation is needed because it clauses are legally prior to any other legislation or court decision. No subsequent bill can invalidate a Constitutional proposition, and no court decision can invalidate one. Those propositions, however, are primarily devoted to defining the organization of the government, to defining the rights and powers of the various branches, and to defining the process by which various high officers are to be chosen. Our Constitution fixes things like the number of senators from each state and the order of succession to the presidency in the event a president dies or becomes incapacitated. None of these concerns human rights, although the organization so defined impinges on the rights of the people. Above all, it becomes a human right of the citizen—a right of citizenship—that the government will faithfully follow the Constitution.

The original Constitution did not address human rights at all, although it was generally accepted that it would be accompanied by some sort of statement of rights. Sixteen of the twenty-seven amendments do address personal rights: the first ten amendments, amendments from thirteen to fifteen which were added as a result of the Civil War, and several more recent amendments dealing with voting rights.[1] Even the latter amendments treat organizational aspects of the government—defining who is entitled to vote—rather than fundamental human rights as that term is usually understood.[2] Broadly speaking, the Constitution exists to define the form of government that a nation has chosen and the terms of the legal process—elections, branches of government, and so on—that embodies and implements the chosen form.

The Right of Privacy

The right of privacy is an integral part of the relationship between the state and the public, and no nation can be considered democratic or limited without it. It is essentially a brake on the discretion of the state that guarantees to the citizens one kind of freedom, a freedom that seems increasingly to be jeopardized in the U.S. today. The people have the right to go about their daily affairs without being subjected to the supervision of the state. This is an unmistakable implication of the proposition that the state is the creation of the people and exists to serve them. There are other political traditions in which this order is reversed, where the citizens exist to serve the state. Even in those places the simple logistics of daily supervision accord to the public a high degree of privacy. It is simply impractical to take it away. That is some consolation, but when the state claims the authority to supervise the people on any point, at the discretion of the state, the people live always under the threat of invasion of their private liberty.

As a case in point, the regulations of the Chinese government having to do with the number of children a family is permitted are unjustified invasions of the privacy of the people. No state has the authority to impose the family choices of any of the citizens. The numbers of citizens, whether large and growing or small and shrinking, are decided by the individual wishes of the people. The state has no authority in this area, and certainly has no authority to try to manipulate the outcome. The state was formed by the people to serve their needs; the people were not formed at birth to serve it. If the heads of the state find the number of citizens either depressingly small or oppressively large is really quite irrelevant. If any one of them is unwilling to serve the public as it stands and prefers some very different population, that governor is entirely free to address his discomfort by resigning his post. If that does not soothe his mind adequately, he is further free to migrate to any country whose population density suits his tastes.

The right of privacy is an integral part of the grant of limited government. What it does not do is to change the nature of the actions that the public engages in. A simple example will make this point. It happens from time to time—I will not speculate on the frequency except to note that it is much higher than we would like to think—that distraught wives dispose of their offending husbands by means of a diet of arsenic milk shakes. They are in reality free to do so because it happens in the private quarters of their homes, hidden from the eyes of the law. That is according to the right of privacy. The old boy's death is still murder, but the judgement has been made that it is preferable to permit a few wives to dispose of their husbands rather than to oppress the vast majority of wives who don't. To repeat, the right of privacy does not in any way change the legality of the actions that occur under its protection. If any wife finds such a quiet, uneventful murder not to her taste, but prefers to hit the old boy with a volley of .45-caliber rounds at the intersection of Hollywood and Vine, the law is not going to be so tolerant. That is because public places are not in fact private, and no right of privacy attaches.

No one can describe himself as "conservative" who questions the right of privacy. Political conservation is defined by the grant of limited government, and more broadly by the rule of subsidiarity which fixes limits on the rights and powers of every element of society. The outcry raised by so-called "conservatives" against the right of privacy clearly identifies them as not conservatives, but totalitarians.

On Roe vs. Wade

The Roe decision by the Supreme Court is in error, but not because it draws upon the right of privacy. The court in that decision, moreover, correctly saw that privacy does not enter into the case. The right of privacy provides a justifiable umbrella covering what are termed "back alley" abortions. While every elective abortion is murder, some murders have to be permitted in the interests of limiting the scope of the government. It is a choice, and in my opinion it is the right choice for the court to have made.

The error in Roe is that they applied the logic of one case to facts from a completely different case, and in the process raised the implication that there is a right to abortion. The facts of Roe are that Ms. Roe asked a Texas court to issue a injunction directing her obstetrician, Dr. Wade, to perform or order an elective abortion in violation of the laws of Texas. Dr. Wade was reluctant to do so, and cited the law as the basis for his refusal. The Roe decision overturned the law in Texas and elsewhere that banned elective abortion. The decision was rendered on the grounds that a doctor can be compelled to satisfy his patient's wishes on the matter of abortion. Now, it is one thing to rule that the patient has the right to force her doctor to do what she wishes, but it is an entirely different thing to find this right in the right of privacy. Nothing could be less private than dragging the obstetrician into court and asking the court to impose its will on him. The right of privacy also does not apply in other ways. According to the logic of Roe, a hospital cannot refuse to provide facilities for abortions, even though there is absolutely nothing private in a hospital.

As it often does, the Supreme Court managed to invalidate the Roe decision even as it affirmed it. The reality of the law is that doctors and hospitals are not compelled to perform elective abortions. The abortions that are now frighteningly frequent take place in specialized abortion facilities, staffed by persons willing to perform them. That quite arguably satisfies the requirements of a right of privacy, replacing the back alley with a store front, and the legal status of abortion is close to what it was before Roe. The false claim to have found a right to elective abortion, however, has by constant repetition and by the willing advocacy of a small elite of society changed personal attitudes toward abortion. Coupled with the corrosive effects of poverty and backwardness and of the removal of protection of marriage, advertising a right to abortion has radically lowered the moral barriers to abortion and made it more frequent.

Subsequent decisions of the court have wandered much farther onto the ice by coming ever closer to finding a right to elective abortion. The doctrine of privacy has become correspondingly irrelevant to the progression of decisions. This represents a radical departure from Roe. The Roe decision is consistent with almost any view on the legality of elective abortion. It is consistent with the view that elective abortion is murder. The logic of the decision is that no matter what the law is regarding elective abortion, the actual practice of it is exempt from legal overview as long as it is carried out in private. That ruling, as I have explained above, is faulty because elective abortions have become such a widespread and grave social problem that the needs of the society must overcome the right of privacy on this point. While faulty, however, Roe is by no means illogical or in violation of settled reasoning. The subsequent decisions that increasingly assert a right to elective abortion, by contrast, are in direct contradiction to the guarantee of the right to life which is recognized in the Declaration of Independence. The Constitution and the Declaration of Independence, which has the same legal status as the Constitution, are above judicial review. It is beyond the power of any court to overturn any part of them. Thus regardless of the personal preferences of the justices, the guarantee of the right to life is the law.

Other Recent Issues of Constitutional Interpretation

Two other matters have arisen recently that highlight fundamental errors of judicial reasoning: one regarding the permissibility of the Pledge of Allegiance and one regarding marriage.

"One Nation under God"

The Pledge of Allegiance is a statement by the people of their loyalty to and reverence for their nation. Courts have allowed themselves to be dragged into a dispute between the majority of American who espouse the pledge as written and a minority who object to the description of the nation as being "under god." As a matter of law, this matter is very simple. It is the right of every American to pledge allegiance to the nation that he or she reveres. Those who are in allegiance with the nation under god have the right to pledge that and those who are in allegiance with a different nation can pledge that. The governing principle in this case has nothing to do with gods or allegiances. The governing principle is the rights of free speech and free conscience. The nation under god is the one that I pledge allegiance to. That is my allegiance. I don't need to secure the permission of any court or any judge to pledge allegiance to that nation. If moreover the parents of small children want their children to be taught allegiance to that same nation, it is their prerogative as parents to teach it. If the schools in a given district wish to serve the children and their parents, they will undertake to make that a lesson in the schools. Parents and children who do not pledge allegiance to the nation under god are entitled to all the same freedoms and rights as is everyone else, and they are entitled to the highest degree of toleration of their views. They are not free, however, to impose their will on their neighbors who constitute a majority. To do that would be the same as for a minority to impose its religious beliefs on the majority.

What the courts have forgotten when they ban the reciting of the pledge in public schools is that the grant of limited government also limits them. They are simply exceeding their authority. The task of courts and the judiciary is to resolve disputes. It is not their job to define religious orthodoxy and to impose it on the people. Now, the dispute between "under god" and "no god" is a true dispute that seems on its face to be sort that judges are asked to resolve, but it differs from the usual ones however in that there are no rights which guide the court. I have the right to pledge allegiance to the nation I hold allegiance to, and everyone else has the same right, even if they are different nations. On a different level, I am a parent and an owner of the public schools that serve my children. I therefore have the right to insist that the public schools teach the important lessons of life, because they are obliged to educate my children and their neighbors. It is not an easy thing for any court to weigh this issue, but the way is made only harder if it refuses to acknowledge the right of every citizen to freedom of conscience and freedom of speech.

Imagine that there was a third party to this dispute, which objected to the characterization of the United

States of America as being "with Liberty and Justice for All." These folks pledge allegiance to America—perhaps with or perhaps without god, we don't know—but are deeply offended by the claim that there is liberty and justice for all. They want to rewrite the pledge to strike out that offending phrase. Now we happen to think that there is liberty and justice for all, and they don't. We are in effect pledging allegiance to different nations. We would have three nations and three allegiances. Each party is free to pledge allegiance as long as they do not attack their neighbors, and if any of the three is in charge of the public schools in an area, they have the right to insist that the schools teach civic virtue according to their vision of it. It would be very instructive, I think, to let a court deal with this issue.

The Definition of Marriage

The Supreme Court of the Commonwealth of Massachusetts recently ruled that they have the power to define marriage in any way they please, because the definition of marriage is not present in either their state constitution or in the federal constitution. The folly of that decision is overwhelmingly obvious. It could be characterized as intellectual dishonesty masquerading as idiocy.

It constitutes a fundamental misunderstanding of what a constitution is. A constitution is not a summary of the law. In fact, as explained, it may be only tangentially related to the rights and freedom of the citizens. To say that we looked all through the relevant constitutions and could not find a definition of marriage is like saying that I looked and looked all over my back yard but still could not find the city of New York. New York is somewhere else, and so is the definition of marriage. The failure of this reasoning is evident also when we apply it to other matters. Nowhere in either constitution is there any definition of "human being." If the justices are reasoning rightly it follows that they are free to define "human beings" any way they please.

Here again we see a court unwilling to recognize the limitations that limited government impose on the court itself. Defining marriage and defining humanity are simply not powers that the public has delegated to the courts. We know what a marriage is, and we know what a human being is. These are known because we are the human beings, and these are our marriages. We have established our government to preserve and defend those realities, and we are not impressed by any court that refuses to do its job. The Constitution is never above the rights and freedoms of the people; it is only the document that lays out how it plans serve them. In the hands of the Supreme Court of Massachusetts, their state constitution and the federal constitution have become instruments not of limited government, but of totalitarian government. There is a famous proverb that tells us where that leads:

> Power corrupts, and absolute power corrupts absolutely.
>
> —Lord Acton

Conclusion

It would the very height of irony for the Constitution of the United States, which rests so clearly on a foundation of natural rights and limited government, to be turned into a pseudo-religious idol, an object of unthinking adulation, used to justify a denial of human rights and a totalitarian government.

Notes

1. The Nineteenth Amendment granting feminine suffrage, the Twenty-fourth nullifying a poll tax (a poll tax is a fee that must be paid in order to cast a ballot), and the Twenty-sixth extending the suffrage to every citizen eighteen years or older.
2. I accept that in some circles this characterization might be controversial, but it is a tangential matter in any case.